T0358208

Cambridge Elements ☰

Elements in Applied Linguistics
edited by
Li Wei
University College London
Zhu Hua
University College London

A SEMIOTICS OF MUSLIMNESS IN CHINA

Ibrar Bhatt
Queen's University Belfast

CAMBRIDGE
UNIVERSITY PRESS

Shaftesbury Road, Cambridge CB2 8EA, United Kingdom

One Liberty Plaza, 20th Floor, New York, NY 10006, USA

477 Williamstown Road, Port Melbourne, VIC 3207, Australia

314–321, 3rd Floor, Plot 3, Splendor Forum, Jasola District Centre, New Delhi – 110025, India

103 Penang Road, #05–06/07, Visioncrest Commercial, Singapore 238467

Cambridge University Press is part of Cambridge University Press & Assessment, a department of the University of Cambridge.

We share the University's mission to contribute to society through the pursuit of education, learning and research at the highest international levels of excellence.

www.cambridge.org
Information on this title: www.cambridge.org/9781009462679

DOI: 10.1017/9781009415910

First published 2023

A catalogue record for this publication is available from the British Library

ISBN 978-1-009-46267-9 Hardback
ISBN 978-1-009-41589-7 Paperback
ISSN 2633-5069 (online)
ISSN 2633-5050 (print)

A Semiotics of Muslimness in China

Elements in Applied Linguistics

DOI: 10.1017/9781009415910
First published online: December 2023

Ibrar Bhatt
Queen's University Belfast

Author for correspondence: Ibrar Bhatt, i.bhatt@qub.ac.uk

Abstract: This Element examines the semiotics of Sino-Muslim heritage literacy in a way that integrates its Perso-Arabic textual qualities with broader cultural semiotic forms. Using data from images of the linguistic landscape of Sino-Muslim life alongside interviews with Sino-Muslims about their heritage, the author examines how signs of 'Muslimness' are displayed and manipulated in both covert and overt means in different contexts. In so doing the author offers a 'semiotics of Muslimness' in China and considers how forms of language and materiality have the power to inspire meanings and identifications for Sino-Muslims and understanding of their heritage literacy. The author employs theoretical tools from linguistic anthropology and an understanding of semiotic assemblage to demonstrate how signifiers of Chinese Muslimness are invoked to substantiate heritage and Sino-Muslim identity constructions even when its expression must be covert, liminal, and unconventional.

Keywords: Chinese Muslims, China, literacy studies, Islam, linguistic ethnography

ISBNs: 9781009462679 (HB), 9781009415897 (PB), 9781009415910 (OC)
ISSNs: 2633-5069 (online), 2633-5050 (print)

Contents

1 Introduction

Sino-Muslims and Their Heritage Literacy

Both the Islamic and Chinese civilisations might appear, to the casual onlooker, to be very distinct and with their own histories and propensities to grow and assimilate other peoples. What happens, though, when elements of both cultures converge over an extended period in a single location? And what kinds of semiotic phenomena might one discover in such a context? When it comes to harmonising their faith within an historically Confucianist and Taoist milieu, as well as more recent Sino-nationalist and even Sino-Marxist sensibilities, the non-Turkic and largely Sinophone Muslims[1] of China have, for many, come to demonstrate a process by which a community can adapt and integrate elements of very different cultural identities in their everyday practice with language and materiality.

In this Element, I examine how this kind of plurality is embodied in the semiotic practices of Sino-Muslim heritage literacy. The data I draw on are part of a corpus of images, interview transcripts, and literacy artefacts amassed as part of the 'Literacy and Harmony' project funded by the Leverhulme Trust and conducted with a team of researchers across China. It incorporates images from the linguistic landscape of Sino-Muslim life, including through the scriptural art of Sino-Islamic calligraphy[2] (or 'Sini Calligraphy'), food heritage practices (including restaurant signs and 'qingzhen'[3] food packaging), and narrative-focussed interviews with Sino-Muslims about heritage literacy in their lifespan and everyday lives. I examine how Islamo-Arabic textual qualities and material signifiers are integrated in these data as part of heritage praxis, and argue that this can add much to an understanding of Sino-Muslim heritage literacy and its expressive potential as a long-standing and ongoing confluence of cultures (namely Chinese and Islamic). I attempt to understand how both textual and visual signs of 'Muslimness' are displayed and manipulated in both covert and overt means to enter into a complex constitutive relation with other categories of social meaning, and how, as materiality, they construct ways to (re-)contour public spaces for Chinese Muslims, configure identity work in the face of censorship of religious expression, and

---

[1] Following Lipman (1997) I will continually refer to China's non-Turkic Sinophone Muslims as 'Sino-Muslims', though I will occasionally use the PRC minzu ethnonym 'Hui' when highlighting post-1950 contexts (see section titled 'A History of Vernacularisation' for a more detailed discussion). Prior to 1950, the term 'Huihui' was generally used to refer to all Muslims in China, and, during the Yuan and Ming dynasties, also used to refer to Persian Christians and Jews.

[2] Sometimes referred to as zhōngguó ālābó wén shūfǎ (中国阿拉伯文书法) or 'Sini Calligraphy'.

[3] This term relates to food that is not just 'halal' but that which is characteristically tied to Sino-Muslim heritage and ethics (see Section 3), and sometimes even colloquially referred to as 'Muslim food'.

provide an access point into better understanding everyday heritage literacy adaptation within China and beyond its shores.

The research is situated within the tradition of literacy studies, which conceptualises literacy primarily as a socially situated semiotic practice (Street 1984; Gee 2008). This necessitates a research process which foregrounds an understanding of the multiple dimensions that heritage literacy plays in the lives of Sino-Muslims, their religio-cultural history, and material culture. However, in a study such as this I must also recognise the complementary domains and sub-literatures with which I must converse in order to establish theoretical foundations. Given the multifaceted nature of ethnic heritage and religion in China, in the following subsections I orient the reader to the particularities of the Sino-Muslim context and history. Much of this research occurs within the fields of Hui Studies[4] (回族研究; huízú yánjiū), which exists under Sinology in many parts of the world, Ethnology (民族学; mínzú xué) within China, and also at the margins of the field of Islamic Studies.

This is then followed by a brief discussion about how I have conceptualised heritage literacy within the study, my deployment of theoretical tools from work in linguistic anthropology, and how this is complemented with ideas around the notion of *semiotic assemblage* (Pennycook 2018). That is to say, while this is a study of literacy, the kinds of practices I try to understand are accomplished through a coalescence of semiotic items rather than just language and texts that occur in public and, as shown in the latter part of the Element, within liminal spaces. These items in various ways *assemble* Muslimness, but in ways that must remain sensitive to the fluid negotiations of meaning-making across modes such as images, cuisine, attire, spatial distribution, artefacts, history, among other things, rather than at the level of individual linguistic actors.

A History of Vernacularisation

To understand the semiotics of Sino-Muslim heritage as it exists today requires an understanding of the community's history and how heritage practices have been shaped over several centuries of cultural production, much of which is impacted by conflict, assimilation, and mobility. Sino-Muslim history and heritage is marked by its continual indigenising impulse and, in Petersen's (2018) terms, forms of *vernacularisation*.[5] Building on arguments made by

---

[4] Hui Studies is an inter-disciplinary field that encompasses sociology, anthropology, and religious studies, and not solely focused on historical or ethnic studies. See Journal of Hui Muslim Minority Studies: https://oversea.cnki.net/knavi/JournalDetail?pcode=CJFD&pykm=HZYJ.

[5] One could argue that all forms of Muslim heritage are marked by an indigenising impulse, sustained by Islamic Law's doctrine of '*urf*, or the incorporation of local customs and norms into the framework of Sacred Law, though acknowledgement of this theological aspect is largely

Flueckiger in her book on gender and vernacular Islam in South Asia, Petersen argues that 'vernacularization points to modes of identification, interpretation, and dialogue that simultaneously advocate local frameworks while advancing universal ideals'. (Petersen 2018, p. 29)

For Sino-Muslims, how semiotic practice occurs today is tied to agentive forms of continual heritage adaptation through political climates in China's history which have not always been favourable to the community. Not only have Sino-Muslims had to respond to historical change and cultural norms imposed upon them, but their heritage practices are also far removed from what many might perceive as Islam's geographical and civilisational centres[6] and, there-fore, susceptible to being deemed as syncretic or derivative. This subsection is a brief overview of some of the historical factors that have caused Sino-Muslim semiotic practices – occurring in and through a wider framing of heritage literacy – to become vernacularised as forms of self-fashioning and performa-tive production shaped and expressed over changing circumstances. This is by no means a detailed historical outline of Sino-Muslim literary history. For such reviews one should consult the works of Petersen (2018), Leslie et al. (2006), and Lipman (1997), among others.

The earliest documentary evidence of Muslim interaction with the Chinese comes during the Tang dynasty (618–907 CE). In *The Old Book of Tang* it is recorded that in 651 a delegation of people from the nascent Arabian empire visited the Tang Court (Bai and Yang 2002). According to the renowned Sino-Muslim historian Bai Shouyi (in Bai and Yang 2002, p. 197), this visit marked the beginning of sustained diplomatic exchanges. As diplomatic and trade relationships solidified with further visits at the behest of various caliphs so too did Muslim social, religious, military, and linguistic connections with China (Yang 1981, pp. 53–4). Notably, Caliph al-Mansur promised a huge battalion of soldiers to support the Tang forces to re-capture the Tang Empire's twin capitals of Chang'an (now named Xi'an) and Luoyang. After the war, the soldiers remained at the behest of the Tang emperor, and inter-married and settled within the local communities. The descendants of these Arab warriors are thought to be the ancestors of a substantial demographic of Sino-Muslims in China's Northwest (Gladney 1998).

---

absent in much Western anthropological and historical work on Sino-Muslims. For more details see Abd-Allah's (2006) essay *Islam and the Cultural Imperative* and Murad's (2020) book *Travelling Home*.

[6] A salient example is within Vincent Monteil's book *Aux cinq couleurs de l'islam* (The Five Colors of Islam), in which he considers five Islamic civilisational centres, manifested in Turkey, Africa, the Malay Archipelago, Arabia, and the Indo-Persian regions. Despite being one of the oldest continuous Islamic cultures with roots stretching as far back as the first century of the Islamic period, Monteil makes no mention of a Sino-Islamic or East Asian Islamic culture.

Aside from diplomatic envoys and military personnel, Muslim merchants from Central Asia and Arabia also began to play an important role in China's commercial life, particularly along the 'Silk Road'[7] and at port cities on the country's southern coast (Lipman 1997). These foreign Muslim traders brought spices and cuisine, ivory, jewellery, and medicines from their home countries, as well as exported Chinese silk, tea, and porcelain (Yang 1981). They contributed significantly to the empire's tax revenues and benefitted from a generally friendly foreign policy during the Tang and Song dynasties. As with the newly settled Muslim soldiers, they were able to marry, have property, worship, and communicate in their native languages though within confined foreign quarters. They thus played an important role in the transmission of Islamic culture and learning to China, bringing Perso-Arabic script, infusing art and calligraphy with their own motifs, influencing architecture and attire, and planting the seeds of a new literate citizenry.

Over generations these communities became more and more assimilated into Chinese society with vernacularised systems of literacy emerging through religious education and the work of traders. For example, an orthographic exchange in form of 'xiaojing' (小经) emerged, a method of transliterating the Chinese language using Arabic script. This was an 'Arabized form of Chinese characters' or 'Pinyin with Arabic' (Qurratulain and Zunnorain 2015, p. 54) which is said to have been formed as Arab traders penned the names of places and people in Arabic, which later developed into a system used for purposes of community correspondence and religious learning. As settlement led to the development of an active literate Muslim culture, xiaojing became a method for students to take notes as mosque teachers elaborated upon Arabic and Persian literature in religious education (Qurratulain and Zunnorain 2015). Sino-Muslim literati were thus able to develop a linguistically flexible system of mosque education called 'scripture hall education' (经堂教育; jīng táng jiàoyù), which consisted of an Islamic curriculum of Arabic, Persian, and Chinese texts to teach Islamic religious subjects to Sino-Muslims who were exclusively Sinophone.

The Mongol invasions and subsequent Yuan dynasty rule (1271–1368) jettisoned Muslim soldiers and literati from the periphery and into an administrative class in Chinese society, which in turn resulted in their spread across the country. During this period, and into the subsequent Ming dynasty (1368–1644), Islamic calligraphy and Perso-Arabic inscription began to appear upon the iconic blue and white porcelain of the imperial court (Frankel 2018).

---

[7] A trans-Eurasian network of trade routes connecting East Asia to Central Asia, India, Southwest Asia, the Middle East, and Europe, though imagined quite differently by the West, Middle East, and China.

Craftsmen sometimes even imitated Islamic religious formulae for fashionable intent, and in ways that no longer yielded any meaning (Schimmel 1984). During the Yuan and very early Ming periods Muslim literati, communities, and religious activities were highly visible in China. Thus, scripture hall education and its resultant literature, as well as the teachers who produced and taught it, are valuable resources in understanding the origins of contemporary heritage literacy practices and for how intellectual networks and literary exchanges occurred in Sino-Muslim communities.

Under the later Ming dynasty, the status of Sino-Muslims began to change radically through imperial edicts which prohibited their social and cultural exclusivity. This resulted in their assimilation into wider Chinese society and culture, including increased adoption of Chinese surnames. By this time, Arabic and Persian had gradually and increasingly faded as languages of everyday spoken and written usage. Chinese was used to translate Islamic texts and to assist in teaching Arabic in Persian, often via transliteration using Chinese characters to approximate Arabic and Persian pronunciations (the inverse of xiaojing), with variance of characters used depending on local dialects and accents.

Further assimilation followed under the Qing dynasty (1636–1912). The Manchu rulers of Qing also preferred Confucian literati over their Muslim counterparts, and Sino-Muslim scholarship overall undertook a more assimilationist turn. This paved the way for the natively Chinese canon of Islamic literature known as the 'Han Kitab',[8] of which the publication of Liu Zhi's 1710 work on the 'Laws and Rites of Islam' (天方典礼; Tianfang Dianli) is considered to be a pivotal moment (Ben-Dor Benite 2005). In Tianfang Dianli, Liu Zhi outlines Islamic Law through a Neo-Confucian language of description. According to Petersen (2018), Sino-Muslim intellectual elites of the late Ming and early Qing dynasties, such as Liu Zhi, were driven to overcome the Sino-Muslim social and intellectual isolation of past generations and develop systems for combining their Islamic and Chinese heritages through the production of religious literature. Petersen goes on to state that 'It was through the inclusion of Chinese as a discursive Islamic language and the development of an official system to spread localized Islamic knowledge that the *Han Kitab* literature began to take shape'. (Petersen 2018, p. 34)

It is not the purpose of this Element to look closely at the Han Kitab corpus, though it is essential in understanding how a contemporary semiotics of Muslimness can take shape upon its shoulders and lingual power. The Han

---

[8] A bilingual coinage of the Chinese word 'Han', referring to Chinese, along with the Arabic word 'kitab' which means 'book', to together constitute a literary genre of Islamic texts in the Chinese language.

Kitab established new horizons of authority in the development of Sino-Muslim heritage, and religious language used throughout the corpus is prevalent today in everyday heritage literacy practices.

As the Republic of China was created (1911–1949), Sino-Muslims, or the 'Hui', were accorded equal recognition as one of China's officially recognised four non-Han ethnic groups.[9] This allowed their socio-economic and cultural position to change and strengthen somewhat, leading to links with Muslim communities outside of China, and the resurgence of their literate culture.

After the Communist Party's victory in 1949, religion was no longer considered a criterion of social identification for China's Muslims. Instead, the new administration assigned fifty-five minority ethnic (少数民族; shǎoshù mínzú) identities upon all non-Han Chinese and promoted its new minzu paradigm through various means, including social incentives (Mullaney 2011). An ethno-religious identity was thus assumed for Sino-Muslims on account of historical ancestral commitment to Islam (Frankel 2021), resulting in religious identity and heritage being considered coterminous with ethnic group (minzu) identity. In particular, for those ethnic groups that identified themselves as 'Muslim' and/or who have a purported religio-cultural association with Islam. While theology was eschewed as an identity marker, a new pan-Hui identity was allowed to emerge within China for those who considered Mandarin (and/or their local *hanyu* dialect) as their primary language. Building on arguments from Gladney (2004), Bhatt and Wang (2023) outline:

> Among China's Muslim *minzu* were some communities who became identified through what was deemed their own language, and from which their PRC designated ethnonym was subsequently derived. These communities include the Uighur, Kzakh, and Tajik ... The label *Hui*, therefore, became legitimated for those who were perhaps the most elusive to define ... As Sinophone Muslims, or Sino-Muslims, they could not be identified by region or a separate language. (Bhatt and Wang 2023, p. 79)

The new Communist administration, initially, brought some favourable improvements for Sino-Muslims, including religious freedom guaranteed by law, and mosques being allowed to continue operating. Regional autonomy was even granted in some areas, most significantly the Ningxia Hui Autonomous Region. Ultimately, however, the regime, like its predecessors, found itself unable to tolerate what it saw as the self-regulating tendencies of the Hui minority, and so it pursued

---

[9] The *zhonghua minzu* policy was established during the early twentieth century to include Han people (the majority ethnic group) alongside four major non-Han ethnic groups: the Manchus, the Mongols, the Hui (ethnic groups of Islamic faith), and the Tibetans, under the notion of a republic of Five Peoples of China (五族共和; wǔzú gònghé) advocated by Sun Yat-sen and the Chinese Nationalist Party (see Gladney 2004, p. 15).

policies to stifle Hui cultural development, shutting down religious schools and Sufi orders, and imprisoning religious leaders in 're-education' camps. As eventually all religious activities were outlawed and institutions were disbanded during the Cultural Revolution (1966–1976), things only became worse. The assault upon Chinese Islam's material and literate culture was severe, and the religion overall had to respond by going underground (Lipman 1997; Frankel 2021).

The government softened its stance on religion after the Cultural Revolution. Today, while Sino-Muslims experience a form of religious freedom (i.e. of belief), this remains closely monitored and religious expression in public realms is rigorously censored and regulated. The liberalisation of economic policies has paved the way for Sino-Muslims to develop their own forms of 'ethnic entrepreneurialism' by leveraging their Muslim identity as a form of 'symbolic capital' (Bourdieu 1986). Urban enclaves such as Muslim Street in Xi'an, the Chengdong District of Xining, and Litong in Wuzhong are awash with heritage-related businesses including food vendors selling 'Muslim food' (see Section 3). These Sino-Muslim areas have contributed to the cultural and economic expansion of Sino-Muslim cuisine and national brands which, according to Chinese anthropologist and sociologist Fei Xiaotong, as cited by Gladney (2004), is reminiscent of the community's origins who nurtured their skills of business and enterprise for centuries along the ancient Silk Road.

While Sino-Muslim commercial place-making (see Section 3) and consumption patterns seem to flourish, other heritage-related domains such as religious education can be subject to different sets of conditions. This contradictory nature of Chinese–Muslim hybridity – or as I prefer to call it herein, *simultaneity* – defines how their heritage literacy practices have emerged historically and where, and how, they manifest today. China's Sino-Muslims thus present a complex entry point into understanding the intricacies of identity and how a semiotics of religion can manifest in the face of historical turbulence and censorship on religious expression. Much has been written about the Hui as a Sino-Muslim minority in China and their cultural and literary history (some of which is referenced earlier). How Muslimness is encoded within the semiotic features of their unique heritage literacy is an important line of inquiry which adds to the body of work.

Islam and Chinese Publics Today

How the religious heritage of Sino-Muslims is manifested in public has become a major political issue in China in the years since the imperative to 'sinicise'[10]

---

[10] 'Sinicisation' is the official Chinese English translation of the term 'zhōngguó huà' (中国化).

religion was announced in May 2015, and then formally inserted as nationwide policy in April 2016 (Madsen 2020). This meant that all parts of Chinese culture (including religion, academia, and the arts) must align with the Chinese characteristics of a socialist society. A particular component of the policy to sinicise religion has been surrounding the design of mosques, public displays of religious signage (which, for Sino-Muslims, are sometimes Perso-Arabic in format), and bans on prayer inscription on Muslim houses in some areas (Gan 2018; Ridgeon 2020).

Pressure imposed on Sino-Muslim communities to conform to the requirements of the state, particularly for those located in the outer provinces of Yunnan, Ningxia, and Qinghai, is not at the same level as that which has been exerted on Uighur communities in the Xinjiang Uighur Autonomous Region. Nevertheless, all Muslim communities in China have had to constantly adapt to evolving forms of sinicisation in public spheres, as well as evolving digital infrastructures of censorship and surveillance in more private spheres (Ho 2018; Wang 2022). This policy has, of course, impacted how heritage manifests in public spaces where long-standing practices have come into direct conflict with state-enforced measures to sinicise religion. It is thus an important question to investigate how Sino-Muslims adapt and attempt to maintain their day-to-day heritage practices and how a semiotics of Muslimness continues to manifest in such a climate.

Theoretical Orientations

The study of how language manifests in public spaces and through material culture, and how it is a window into a community's ethnolinguistic vitality, is largely attributable to theoretical and methodological approaches developed in the work on linguistic landscaping. The early work of Landry and Bourhis (1997) drew attention to the signage in particular locales. Later work (see Shohamy and Gorter 2009; Shohamy et al. 2010) began to incorporate material objects and sounds, in addition to the collection of locally based signage, to construct an understanding of how public spaces are linguistically, and thereby symbolically, constructed.

Studies in linguistic anthropology in different contexts have further shown that religiosity can be expressed through multiple manifestations that often shift over time, place, and across linguistic systems (e.g. Shandler 2006; Ahmad 2011; Avni 2014). Work on religious linguistic landscapes has shown that members of a religious community can utilise a script normally used for a different language, such as Urdu written in Devanagari rather than its usual Perso-Arabic script (see Ahmad 2011). Group members can also engage in 'bivalency', the deployment of linguistic elements that belong within two named languages at the same time (see Benor 2020). In each case these are facets of 'translingual practice' (Canagarajah 2013), where group members will strategically navigate use of multiple languages and codes as one complete repertoire. *Heritage literacy*, as I attempt to define it, must therefore be seen as a linguistically dynamic social practice rather than based on a static linguistic system.

In the field of literacy studies (Heath 1983; Street 1984; Barton 2007; Gee 2008), which has links to linguistic anthropology (Gumperz and Hymes 1972) and linguistic ethnography (Tusting 2013), literacy is conceptualised as embedded within social and cultural activity. Important early work in the field, as the analytic paradigm evolved, focussed heavily on the literacy practices within particular religious communities. For example, studies such as Scribner and Cole's (1981) on the literacy practices of the Vai in Liberia, and Street's (1984) fieldwork in Iran both investigated how Quranic literacy is transmitted in various social and cultural contexts alongside other literacies prevalent in the lives of group members. Further studies have also shown how religious literacies can be used to socialise group members into moral value systems (e.g. Baquedano-López 2016), mediate boundaries between, for example, the mosque, school, and the home (e.g. Sarroub 2002), and be differentiated according to language (Martin-Jones and Jones 2000).

I attempt to build on this scholarship, but frame my sphere of concern as heritage literacy, which I consider to encompass, in Sino-Muslim contexts, as 'goal-directed practices of literacy in which heritage and religion have a role' (Bhatt and Wang 2023, p. 85). This allows me a wide scope of practice which can encompass not just religious activities – rooted in heritage knowledge – but also informal and mundane practices of heritage literacy which may be outside the purview of religious institutions, formal education, and state-defined minzu parameters. In a Chinese context, these kinds of heritage practices can be described as occurring within a 'minjian' (民间) or 'among-the-people' sphere of activity. According to Erie (2016) in his extensive study of Sino-Muslims in Linxia in Northwest China, minjian can be considered a middle ground between the Party-State and the Hui community. Here, heritage as cultural material is conventionalised and shoehorned into an 'ideal' (and sometimes policed) Sino-Muslim identity. According to Veg (2019), however, minjian also includes organic and 'grassroots' values, practices, and behaviours which may be neither imposed nor ritualistic. It is here where Sino-Muslims will engage in divergent practices as part of heritage, and invoke personae and semiotic ideologies that are more hybrid than official spaces (be they political or religious) might permit. I thus define the scope of my interest in the heritage literacy of China's

Sino-Muslims as encompassing both individual affective qualities and the politics of representation and difference. This perspective also aligns with a reframing of heritage as presented in the work of Harrison (2013).

Additionally, knowledge that is conveyed and bequeathed via practices of heritage literacy will integrate oral, written, and other (e.g. visual) modes (Rumsey 2010; Bhatt and Wang 2023). It is thus based on embodied semiotic practices, tied to much more than text, and can encompass human performance, history, identity, and place-making. Investigating and theorising heritage literacy and its multi-semiotic reality must therefore be 'from the ground up', and at the level of *everyday practice*.

It is at this level of the *everyday* through which individuals present themselves (Goffman 1959), and 'give off' (Goffman 1959, p. 4) impressions of their identity through various kinds of semiotic work. What becomes important, therefore, in a study such as this is the agency and awareness of Sino-Muslims to create, interpret, emplace, and/or valorise signs that are constitutive of heritage. The notion of 'semiotic ideology' thus lies at the heart of this research, and is defined by anthropologist Webb Keane as 'people's underlying assumptions about what signs are, what functions signs do or do not serve, and what consequences they might or might not produce' (Keane 2018, p. 65). A semiotic ideology is a system of meanings, norms, and values, whether consciously recognised or not, associated with particular modes of signification. According to Keane (2007, 2018), semiotic ideologies are not just abstract ideas, but, rather, they are deeply embedded in everyday language practices and material culture. When Sino-Muslims draw attention to practices of heritage literacy, regardless of its mode of practice or form, they do so because they perceive these practices as having a bearing on something, be it ritual, ideas, consciousness, agency, or the relationships among these. Heritage literacy practices thus function within what Keane calls 'representational economies'. In addition to language, material objects themselves can also serve as vehicles for semiotic ideologies (see Ivanič et al. 2019). For instance, in Keane's (2007) book *Christian Moderns: Freedom and Fetish in the Mission Encounter*, he examines how Christian missionaries in Indonesia promoted a particular semiotic ideology which was also expressed through material objects, such as the Bible, and thereby served as a tangible symbol of the Christian worldview.

My focus on Sino-Muslim heritage literacy in everyday action is thus meant to revive and foreground that which is lost through the institutionalisation of literacy under two dominant paradigms exerting influence upon the lives of contemporary Sino-Muslims. The first is one which ties literacy knowledge and mass-literacy policy exclusively to Standard Mandarin as a key enabler of gaining economic advantage (see Xinhua 2019). Since Sino-Muslims are considered to be historically sinicised, and with no minority language through which their heritage can be ring-fenced and protected, what remains is only their heritage literacy, and new adaptations of everyday practice. The second is related to how Sino-Muslim heritage literacy is far removed from what many might perceive as Islam's geographical and civilisational centres and therefore perhaps perceived as peripheral, or even derivative, as an Islamic culture.

This research is influenced by the cross-cutting body of literature outlined, and offers new theoretical and methodological insights in two ways: First, in my examination of a semiotics of Muslimness I have not just paid attention to physical spaces which are occupied and made meaningful through linguistic and other semiotic means, but also how those very means are adapted and appropriated in the circulation of traditional practices such as Sini calligraphy, the packaging of Sino-Muslim food products, and other notable contexts where heritage literacy emerges as salient in this study. To this end, and building on arguments by Keane (2018) and Pahl and Rowsell (2011), my concern is with how a semiotics of Muslimness intersects with material culture, circulates in society, and is made to not just give meaning to a particular space or product of heritage but also used to fulfil further social, cultural, religious, economic, and political functions. In this kind of environment, a semiotics of Muslimness must move beyond the logocentric approaches of early research to incorporate a broader semiotics, including one which integrates space, place, clothing and images, and as Pahl and Rowsell (2011) put it, 'listening to cultural "stuff" from homes and communities' (p. 492), as within my province of concern. In other words, material culture does not just inform how I come to understand heritage literacy, but it is also integral to the process of semiosis.

Second, considering the sociopolitical context in which this research is conducted and the highly censored and regulated heritage practices of Sino-Muslims in China (outlined in the earlier section), I am also concerned with how these practices are carried out in situations where creative adaptations have become necessary as part of heritage maintenance. For this reason, in the context of China's Sino-Muslims, some practices of heritage literacy constitute what I propose in this Element as *covert semiosis* by virtue that they are not explicitly read as religious by a dominant discourse. Covert semiosis, as I exemplify it in the coming sections, can take place in a particular moment, sometimes in a fleeting manner, and at other times through more calculated semiotic activity. The defining feature of it, however, is that it is 'below the radar' and yet purposefully designed to be *noticed* by a segment of the social world, either through the use of specific semiotic resources or because it occurs in locations that are outside of general public view.

According to Blommaert (2005), semiotic choices, including those which I argue constitute covert semiosis, are 'nested in particular orders of indexicality'. These are unevenly distributed and operate across conventional community boundaries, making them inaccessible to everyone in a given unit of people conceived of as *a* 'society' or 'community' (Blommaert 2005). This aspect is necessary for covert semiosis to be successful as while it sits at the interstices, it can simultaneously appear front-and-centre in public space; it can often be beyond linguistic, and may also be heavily dependent on the signifying power of objects. Through seeking ways to maintain and adapt heritage literacy in spaces that have been targeted for censorship and sinicisation, covert semiosis becomes a possibility and, arguably, has been a long-standing strategy of Sino-Muslims.[11]

The analytic shifts I propose necessitate the use of a wider framework to understand and consider a dialectic relationship between language and materiality and the kinds of adaptations which occur in my context of interest. I therefore attempt to connect these analytic shifts with recent developments in applied linguistics which have highlighted how meaning is constructed in multi-semiotic ways, and through a fluid negotiation of language with other modes including images, bodily movement and sound (Pennycook 2017). Meaning is thus conceptualised in terms of 'spatial distribution, social practices and material embodiment rather than the individual competence of the sociolinguistic actor' (Pennycook 2018, p. 47). Here I deploy Pennycook's framing of semiotic assemblage as used by sociolinguists and applied linguists. There are various schools of semiotics which have addressed multimodality and visual registers, including the work of Barthes (1977), the visual semiotics of Peirce (1934) and Sebeok (1976), and more recent work on *geosemiotics* by Scollon and Scollon (2003). Pennycook, however, sets out his point of departure by drawing on the work of 'posthuman' thought (see Barad 2007; Bennett 2010), through which he argues that analytic attention must shift from anthropocentric accounts alone to 'the greater totality of interacting objects, places and alternative forms of semiosis' (Pennycook 2018, pp. 54–5).

What is also required is an exploration of the spaces in which semiotic material occurs, is conventionalised, and, building on Gourlay et al. (2021), how boundaries are made and unmade in spaces which are characterised by heritage. In doing so we can see how heritage practices can become more permeable, fluid,

---

[11] I noted a possible example of how covert semiosis has occurred historically during a visit to the Hongshuiquan [洪水泉] mosque in rural Qinghai. At the fourteenth-century mosque site I observed that some of the Quranic wall engravings had been erased during the Cultural Revolution, while other engravings remained intact. Upon enquiry, I learned that the surviving Arabic engravings were in Sini script, which has a distinctive Chinese aesthetic. This led the 'Red Guards' at the time of the purge to mistakenly believe they were not Arabic (i.e. scriptural) engravings but decorative patterns, thus sparing them from eradication.

fragmented, and even more difficult to detect as a result of censorship of the linguistic landscape both online and in physical places. There are good reasons for talking about Sino-Muslim heritage literacy in these terms. Semiotic practices related to heritage literacy may end up being subtle and covert performances of religiosity and, as we shall come to see in the context of this research, dispense of any linguistic markers altogether in order to be noticed.

In this respect, and as argued elsewhere (see Bhatt and Wang 2023) the process of entextualisation – the turning of discourse into recontextualised and transportable forms that circulate and in new contexts (Bauman and Briggs 1990) – becomes analytically central to a study of heritage literacy. This potential for language to reproduce and transform across contexts and be subject to recontextualisation can be important in understanding how practices of heritage literacy are maintained, adapted, or relinquished across generations.

Therefore, the key concerns in this Element are how heritage literacy practices exemplify contestations in negotiating boundaries between perceptions of the 'sacred' and the 'profane'.[12] It delves into how a semiotics of Muslimness is circulated in ways that imbue the everyday with sacred meaning and spectral traces of the past, and how religious iconicity is invoked to substantiate heritage, even when its expression must be made covert.

Research Procedure

A combination of research methods was employed in the study, using a team of five researchers located in the United Kingdom and across China, and led by the author. The conception, design, and analysis of the study were guided by the context-sensitive and ethnographic approach to heritage literacy outlined in the previous section. The study's aims to capture the multi-dimensional nature of heritage literacy, and the broader social processes and material actors through which it is embedded led to the following methods:

(1) Images of the linguistic landscape, including shop signs and food packaging, were collected at various sites of the study. Participants also shared important artefacts related to heritage literacy, and communications such as social media posts for deeper probing into their heritage significance via interviews.

(2) Narrative-focussed interviews with Sino-Muslim participants about heritage literacy in the lifespan and in current everyday practice.[13] Sometimes

---

[12] Written in quotations as these are loaded and contested terms, especially in the field of Religious Studies.

[13] While the term 'heritage literacy' was used as the research was introduced, it remained an etic term of investigation and not readily used by respondents.

these were 'go-along' interviews in particular locations where forms of heritage are prominent (e.g. the 'Muslim Street' quarter in Xi'an), and on other occasions they were biographic in nature.

Data were collected by the author and supported by the research team through various field visits in the period between 2019 and 2023. Interviews were undertaken both in person and online, with adaptations made in response to changing pandemic conditions and lockdown policies in China. That is to say, the choice of interview mode was based on what was practicable at the time and sometimes occurred during visits to the field by myself and/or a locally based project researcher. Some of the interviews were carried out in the UK.

All researchers in the team are of Islamic faith and, aside from myself, are either Hui or Han Chinese. This allowed participants to be recruited through a combination of purposive and snowball sampling, building on personal contacts made via locally based networks. This brings me to the potentially thorny issue of 'religious positionality', a somewhat under-addressed matter in Western social research (Rumsby and Eggert 2023). As a Western researcher of Islamic faith and theological education, I was able to establish both a religious and academic common ground with the research team. This common ground extended to many of the participants encountered during the study, and also enabled an auto-ethnographic component as researchers shared their own reflections of their engagement with heritage literacy during the research process. As a result, our collective positionality led to profound and empathetic research encounters with the respondents.

Another issue that needs to be addressed is the challenge of being a religiously ambivalent scholar in a secularised and, at times, theophobic academic environment. As highlighted by Ferber (2006), the issue is especially relevant in studies like this one, where both researchers and participants come from the same faith tradition. In Western academia, there is a prevailing assumption and stigma that researchers who share the same faith tradition as their participants may not be impartial and, therefore, require a kind of 'meth-odological atheism'.[14] However, scholars from various disciplines have demonstrated the explicit advantages of religious positionalities, such as in studies of human geography (Kong 2001), international relations (Rumsby and Eggert 2023), and religious literacy (Rosowsky 2008).

These scholars are part of a growing number who have emphasised that being a member of the same faith community as the one being researched is a crucial

---

[14] On this point, the same criticism could be applied to researchers from the same methodological or ideological persuasion, and so on. Also, religious common ground cannot always be assumed as faith traditions are riven with theological differences, conflict, and sectarianism.

factor for gaining respondent acceptance. Additionally, one's religio-cultural familiarity can deepen research encounters and research-based insights. Researchers' biographies, histories, and identities can thus help shape the research process and influence the representation and legitimation of participants' voices and emic accounts. Engaging with faith communities as *coreligionist-researchers* can offer valuable insights into the complexity of lived experiences, values, and beliefs, and contribute to a more nuanced understanding of the role of faith in people's lives. It was, therefore, a huge asset in this research.

The focal research sites include Xi'an (Shaanxi Province), Wuzhong (Ningxia Province), and Xining (Qinghai Province), which were chosen because of their unique forms of heritage literacy and because individual researchers were based there. Additional elements of the dataset come from other locations and have also been drawn from to augment the analysis in this Element. This includes data from respondents who are from other locations such as Changchun (Jilin Province), Lanzhou and Linxia (Gansu Province), Hangzhou (Zhejiang Province), Shanghai, and even from outside China. Data was also collected from Yunnan and Hong Kong SAR, though this specific data set is not used within this Element.

Interviews were conducted by all researchers in the team, with Mandarin as the dominant medium in most cases, and some interviews in English. Elements of Classical Arabic also emerged when it was needed and helpful during research encounters. My research team's linguistic (including dialect) and religio-cultural familiarity meant that we could engage in a *collective* process of transcription, translation, and editing to check religious terminology and specific language features that vary across regions and sub-communities. This allowed me to include English translations in the text for this Element, along with technical vocabulary and expressions that the participants used in their original Mandarin (written here in simplified characters) alongside diacriticised pinyin in parentheses for clarity. The data collection of transcripts, artefacts, and photographs was then imported into NVivo, followed by a thematic classification procedure that allowed the discovery of patterns within the data (Saldaña 2011). These patterns crystallised into several themes, some of which have guided the content and structure of this Element.

Upon the study's ethical approval,[15] specific ethical dilemmas emerged related to issues of anonymity and identifiable features of participants, and the security risks associated with religious discussions in online platforms (see Weixin 2021). In order to mitigate these, respondents' names and precise

---

[15] Institutional ethical approval was obtained from the Ethics Committee of the School of Social Sciences, Education and Social Work, Queen's University Belfast (REF 171_2021).

locations were anonymised at source (i.e. immediately as the data was collected from them). Permission was granted to use any digital artefacts in this work, and all used artefacts were thoroughly anonymised. Prior to manuscript submission, permission was re-confirmed in writing. Participant pseudonyms in this Element reflect their preferred real name; for example, if a participant preferred a Chinese, Arabic or English name then their pseudonym was chosen to reflect this. For reasons of language ideology in self-naming, I deemed this salient. Following this was another layer of anonymisation, in instances where I considered that identification could occur indirectly through description, as in the hypothetical example 'a notable calligraphy Master from Kunming said ... '. In these particular cases, such descriptions were further generalised to avoid identification. Additionally, interview discussions (particularly when conducted online) remained on topics connected to Hui ethnic heritage, rather than touching on religious proselytisation, and thereby remained within the confines of Chinese law and minimised any risk to respondents.

In the data examined in this Element, textual and visual features of all extracts have been preserved, though identifying characteristics of social media posts have been completely removed. The analysis presented here focuses on salient threads within multiple lines of inquiry which form the basis of the sections that follow: Sini calligraphy, food heritage, and heritage literacy within liminal spaces. Some sub-themes, such as *space*, *boundaries*, *resources*, were relevant across thematic areas, in which case the dominant one became the focus of the analysis.

2 The Semiotics of Sini Calligraphy

Sini Calligraphy as Historical Practice

Sino-Islamic calligraphy is a syncretic practice that integrates both Islamic and Chinese calligraphy traditions. According to Petersen (2018) historical Sino-Muslims used calligraphic art as a form of strategic leverage during the Ming and Qing dynasties, to demonstrate an assimilation of Chinese aesthetics and – via the Han Kitab – Islam's compatibility with Confucianism. Drawing on the work on Sino-Muslim Confucianist Liu Zhi (1670–1724 AD), Petersen argues that Liu presented a wholly Sinic-oriented account of how the Arabic letters of the Quran (including its diacritic features), like Chinese characters, have intrinsic semiotic properties that each point to qualities within reality and therefore to be 'understood as both receptive and creative entities within the cosmos' (p.179). Lui employed a neo-Confucianist[16] and Taoist language of

---

[16] A capacious term to cover the broad Confucianist revival from the early Song dynasty (960–1279) and into the Ming period (1368–1644).

description to make his claims. An organic feature of this broad theological confluence of Sinic and Islamic culture is that two apparently incommensurable orthographic systems (Chinese and Arabic) could be harmoniously merged through creative endeavour: an aesthetic union exemplified in the art of Sini calligraphy.

With the adoption of Chinese material culture as well, Sini script evolved as calligraphers learned to write Arabic using Chinese ink brushes. Sini calligraphy thus provided a firm foundation for the emergence of an indigenous Sino-Muslim heritage within China, and bolstered the Sino-Muslim community's claim to indigenousness and intangible cultural heritage that lasts till today. Sino-Muslims thus developed their own Sini script, which was rounded, sweeping, with thick and tapered effects, and which sometimes appropriated the square forms of Chinese characters (see Figures 1 and 2); very similar to the Chinese calligraphy that they were surrounded by at the time. Importantly, both cultures emphasise calligraphy as part of a refined and esteemed scholarly tradition, and images like that of Figure 2 display how the two scripts are set on an equal footing in Sino-Muslim spaces. This adaptation of the local aesthetic into their script and religious spaces created a unique blend of cultural expression, through which it gains distinctive aesthetic resonance for Chinese Muslims, and a compelling intersection of traditions.

The art form endured in China throughout centuries, despite numerous social upheavals for Sino-Muslims and isolation from other parts of the

Figure 1 The Islamic declaration of faith by Mi Guangjiang, in a square character format turned on its side (photo by author).

Figure 2 Front view of the Xi'an Grand Mosque situated within the Muslim Quarter district of Xi'an. Columns reveal square-character style Arabic calligraphy (photo by author).

Islamic world. This demonstrates the resilience of Sino-Muslim heritage and underscores the vital role of the written word in heritage practices. Therefore, in focussing on these practices within this study, I begin with accounts from two focal participants: Teacher Han and Teacher Li. Over the course of several days, I stayed with them and saw how, in different ways, they are both deeply involved with Sini calligraphy as a religious tradition, and both masters of the art in their own right. Other participants within this account are Sini calligraphy students Qasim, who was based in Türkiye at the time of the data collection, and Baojie, a Han Chinese Muslim from Jilin Province. While research encounters with them were dominated by this particular aspect of heritage, other participants throughout the study drew less on calligraphy heritage and more from various forms of relationship with Perso-Arabic script as part of everyday heritage literacy. These include Meili from Xinjiang (though now based in Hong Kong), and Lei from Xi'an. I have therefore used their accounts to augment the analysis of the focal calligrapher participants where this is necessary. The section ends with a broader discussion of how the Arabic symbolism of Sini calligraphy, is attached to semiotic ideologies and the valorisation of its script as 'jing' (经; scripture/classic).

Entextualising Chineseness

We first turn our attention to how as a confluence of literacy traditions, Sini calligraphy incorporates Chinese philosophy[17] and Islamic elements in both its visual manifestations and procedural methods, as Teacher Li and Teacher Han outline in the following excerpts. Each of them has been involved in Sini calligraphy for over twenty years, and has also studied with reputable Masters and attained authorisation (Ar. 'ijaza) in the art. Both were born and raised in Qinghai Province, and studied within the traditional Sino-Muslim scripture hall education system (see Section 1). It was within these formative mosque-based scripture hall years that they encountered Sini calligraphy and decided to embark upon it as a professional as well as spiritual practice. According to Teacher Han:

> After Islamic calligraphy spread to China, it was combined with our Chinese calligraphy and Taoist culture [道家文化; dàojiā wénhuà]. It is no longer just a religious subject. It is part of China's intangible cultural heritage [非物质文化遗产; fēi wùzhì wénhuà yíchǎn].
>
> Elements of Chinese calligraphy have become incorporated into our Arabic calligraphy. For example, when we write Arabic calligraphy with a Chinese brush pen and in the Chinese method, it is done a particular way. If we write the letter 'waw' [و], then we show the shape of the brush's angle [露锋; lù fēng] at the initial point of contact with the paper. If we write the letter 'alif' [ا] it is not lù fēng but rather we conceal the brush's angle [藏锋; cáng fēng] at the head of the letter. We fulfil all the rules of Chinese calligraphy like this.

Here Teacher Han indicates how he and other Sini calligraphers move the Chinese calligraphy brush (毛笔; máobǐ) after it initially contacts with the paper in line with a number of specific Chinese calligraphic techniques which emphasise an embodied material practice (see Kwo 1990). In the writing of some Arabic letters, the very starting point where the brush touches the paper is visible through showing the shape of the brush's angle (露锋; lù fēng), and sometimes it is hidden (藏锋; cáng fēng). Furthermore, in characteristically Taoist fashion, the showing of the tip of the brush and its concealing is also to allow discerning later generations to interpret the calligrapher's legacy. As Qasim, a student of Sini Calligraphy tells:

> When copying calligraphy, we analyse not only the movement of the letters, but also the life and emotions of the writer. So, hiding and showing the brush tip also has ontological meaning, the hierarchies of existence, and both hidden and manifested realities.

---

[17] By 'Chinese philosophy' I am referring to a range of philosophical principles and sensibilities which, while link to Confucius or Lao Tzu and the Confucian and Taoist schools broadly defined, are actually far wider in scope than either (see Feng and Bodde 1976).

There are two possible implications of this. The first is that the letters take a characteristically Chinese look, as in Figures 1 and 2. The second, is that the art, as a form of writing-art, 'gives off' something about the writer through a series of very subtle meaning effects which Qasim describes through Chinese philosophical terms as 'hierarchies of existence' and 'hidden and manifested realities'. Qasim's latter point relates to space-consciousness, or 'blank-leaving' (留白; liú bái) as a distinct strategy in Chinese art. Next, I will deal with the former implication and then return to the blank-leaving shortly after.

Teacher Han describes this by pointing to the way Sini calligraphy is manifested (at least in his perception) within the areas where 'the Han culture originated':

> Sometimes when I look at the Arabic calligraphy written by the Chinese, it feels different from the calligraphy written by the Arabs. If you go to the Central Plains and Henan, where the Han culture originated, you will see the plaques in the mosques have more intense elements of Chinese calligraphy, though embedded in Arabic. Basically everything, including the composition, arrangement, top-bottom ordering, thickness, weight applied, stroke sequence and speed, are all in accordance with Chinese calligraphic principles. No other country will use this model. Except perhaps for native Japanese Muslims,[18] as they are within our Confucian cultural circle.

In the previous extract Teacher Han tells how Sini calligraphy represents a *longue durée* interaction and syncretism of cultural material. He concludes that the closer one gets to 'the Central Plains ... where the Han culture originated', the less culturally distinct the Sini calligraphy becomes and the less it follows the classical style as developed in the Middle East.[19] This seems to reflect a pattern of greater Sinicisation and assimilation in the heartland of Chinese civilisation than at its periphery. Variations in distinction are not just perceived in terms of process and procedure of writing but, more tangibly, also with the tools used. For instance, Islamic writing in China often deploys a brush. The more widely used 'qalam' (格莱姆; géláimǔ) or 'Pen' used by Arab and Turkish calligraphers was also adopted as a writing tool, and most senior Sini calligraphers are able to use both tools to write, though Chinese calligraphic principles align more naturally with the former (Kwo 1990).

---

[18] A notable Japanese Islamic calligrapher is Fuad Kouichi Honda; see www.arabnews.com/node/1712096/lifestyle.

[19] During my fieldwork, I encountered an individual who had previously served as an Imam in several mosques across Henan. As we delved into a discussion about Quranic recitation, he showcased his recital which bore a resemblance to the rhythmic patterns of Beijing Opera, underscoring a form of linguistic assimilation prevalent in Eastern China.

The integration of principles from Chinese philosophy was also talked about by Teacher Li:

> We express Yin and Yang[20] in the work itself. The Arabic calligraphy written by the Arabs was one stroke followed by another stroke, but the rules of the Chinese people come from Chinese culture . . . The first line you write is Yin, and your second line must be Yang, the first line is short, the second line must be long, it must have symmetry, virtual and real, the first line you go fast, the second line slower. During the slow and fast rhythm, there will be Yin and Yang fluctuations, just like music.

The notion of 'entextualisation' is a useful way for us to study how semiotic principles (in this case Chinese philosophy's complementary forces of Yin and Yang) are performatively lifted out from their original contexts and translated into the fundamentals of brushwork in Sini calligraphy. According to Bauman and Briggs (1990), entextualisation refers to 'the process of making a stretch of our linguistic [or semiotic] production into a unit – a text – that can be lifted out of its interactional setting' (Bauman and Briggs 1990, p. 73). It is realised through decontextualisation, that is to say through lifting discourse material *out* of its original setting, and being recontextualised, or translated and/or adapted *into* a new context and sometimes for an entirely new audience and purpose (see Blommaert 2005; Leppänen et al. 2014). It is thus made into a 'new' discourse and with new metapragmatic frames (Blommaert 2005, p. 252).

As a combination of writing alongside powerful visual symbolism, Sini calligraphy consists of a series of multiple entextualising features. These include the Yin-Yang stroke sequences as outlined by Teachers Han and Li which, when embodied in their calligraphy, makes their works an affirmation of Chinese philosophical precepts. For them, the concept of Yin-Yang is used to balance the elements of Quranic calligraphy work and to create a harmonious composition: The balance between the black (Yin) and white (Yang) space, the weight of the characters, the rhythm of the lines, and the overall balance of the work are all influenced by these principles. By carefully considering the complementary opposites as balance in their work, they aim to create aesthetically resonant Islamic compositions that convey further meaning via Chinese symbolism.

This simplification and repetition becomes an essence of the art, impacting even the economy of line and colour, and also influencing their personal scholar-artist lives as spiritual discipline and frugality are considered essential for the Master. Even the blank spaces of the page are

---

[20] Yin-Yang is a fundamental concept in Chinese philosophy, which represents the duality of nature as fundamental complementary opposites (see Feng and Bodde 1976).

essential in reflecting continual meditations on space-consciousness, or 'blank-leaving', echoing Qasim's account earlier as an important technique in Chinese philosophical and aesthetic traditions.

I also interviewed Baojie, a student of Sini calligraphy from Jilin Province. Baojie is a Han convert to Islam and had been studying the art for two years at the time of the research. The reasons she gave for learning the art echo the accounts provided earlier by the teachers but in ways that point to both her personal life journey and historical identity:

> Sini calligraphy is civilisational. It represents the Islamic civilisation and Chinese civilisation. That is the main reason why I am so moved by it . . . I am reminded of the Quran a lot through calligraphy. It helps with my Arabic learning as I get to practise the letters.

Baojie is new to the Islamic faith and is learning Arabic. Sini calligraphy is an ideal way for her to converge two types of 'civilisation' in her personal life in a way that integrates her Chinese past with her new Islamic present and future. We will see more reference to the term 'civilisation' in various ways throughout this Element (including in Section 4). Baojie's sentiments echo the efforts of historical Sino-Muslim intellectuals, under the late Ming and Qing dynasties, in continually asserting the relevance of Islam with China's affairs and the religion's compatibility with Confucianism and Taoism. As a recent Sino-Muslim, though not 'Hui', Baojie feels that she is a purveyor of Sino-Muslim heritage and must embody the two teachings within herself. Sini calligraphy allows her to do this harmoniously and in a way that does not belabour the disjunctions between her Chineseness and Muslimness. It is thus a site for *simultaneity*.

However, even a nationally recognised form of intangible heritage requires diplomatic language when talked about in public and online spaces. When she speaks about her Sini calligraphy course on Weixin[21] to her Han friends and family, she describes it as a 'personal development course' and avoids going into too much detail about the Quranic verses being written, so as not to attract too much attention to her Islamic conversion.

If teachers Han and Li, and students Qasim and Baojie, were born 1000 years ago, they would be writing the same letters, with the very same set of tools, on the same type of paper, and with the same procedure. As Sino-Muslims, they would also be engaging in the same kinds of dialogue and negotiations about their heritage and how it is embodied through their calligraphic practice. For them, therefore, the creativity of Sini calligraphy is expressed less in innovation

---

[21] Weixin (微信) is the dominant chat application in China and the fourth largest globally. Strictly speaking, 'WeChat' is the name for the same app when registered by users outside of China.

and more through repetition and virtuoso conformity to a rigid set of rules that are Chinese in their origins, though what is written is wholly Islamic and Arabic. What is created is not just the literal outline of the shapes of the Arabic letters but, through ongoing entextualisation, their spirit, and Sino-Islamic essence.

To understand this better, we must consider how such art is deployed by Sino-Muslims in everyday use, as further outlined in the remainder of this section and also in Section 4. We must consider a semiotic ideology that mediates between individuals and their agency (i.e. their ability to act), on the one hand, and of semiotic practices (i.e. how people use those symbols), on the other.

Sini Calligraphy and Digitalisation

The calligraphers in the study also strategically deployed social media and other digital tools, particularly since the COVID-19 pandemic, in order to maintain practice with their students and communities that have emerged through their work. For example, since the pandemic Teacher Li has been conducting classes online and using his Weixin account to promote his calligraphy practice, recruiting students from across the country and some in other countries (including Turkey, the US, and the UK). His social media updates are all calligraphy-related and often with images of his new work, video clips of works in progress, and sometimes spiritual advice and guidance based on the calligraphy presented. Consistent with his Master's approach of incorporating spiritual guidance as part of calligraphy instruction, Teacher Li also integrates advice in his social media posts, though for this he needs to tread carefully due to online censorship laws, as discussed in Section 1. An example is in Figure 3. In this post Teacher Li posts his calligraphic rendition of a brief poem by the eighth-century theologian Imam Al-Shafi.

English translation of Chinese text:	Arabic:	English translation of Arabic:
As long as you have teachings [jiàomén] and good health, do not grieve for what you do not attain in this life. If you fail to achieve any dream that you pursued, your jiàomén and good health are enough to compensate for it. - Don't be sad	لا تأس في الدنيا على فائت وعندك الاسلام والعافية ان فات امرٌ كنت تسعى له فيفهما من فائت كافية	Never be saddened by what you lose in this world, while you have Islam and general wellness. If you lose something that you were rushing towards, then the fact that you lost it is sufficient.

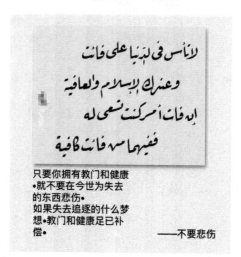

Figure 3 Teacher Li's post (used with permission).

The original Arabic poem mentions 'And you have Islam and general wellness' which Teacher Li renders into something completely different in Chinese. Instead of directly translating the original Arabic in the image, he presents a version that has explicit reference to religion removed. The word 'jiàomén', which roughly relates to 'teachings', replaces the word 'Islam', to write another version altogether. In interview, Teacher Li justified this as the most appropriate word for his online purposes, and that people would understand what is being said. He also wrote a post alongside this image giving advice about the dangers of sadness when worldly ambitions are not achieved, pointing once again to the re-rendering of the message of the poem from its original as a work of calligraphic art, to the translation with redacted elements, and his post which provided elucidation for his followers. Another example of a kind of elision and removal of an explicit religious reference is from Teacher Han's post in Figure 4.

In this post, Teacher Han presents his latest piece, a depiction of a key phrase[22] which is chanted by many Muslims as a form of 'dhikr' (meditative remembrance of God), and considered one of the most important invocations in Islam. The invocation is surrounded by backdrop of a traditional Chinese landscape drawing known as *shanshui* (mountain and water). Shanshui is one of the most widespread and appreciated forms of traditional Chinese art, and is supposed to evoke feelings, ideas and spiritual concepts, rather than a faithful

---

[22] Translation: 'Glory be to Allāh and all praise is due to Him, glory be to Allāh the Magnificent'.

有两种东西丧失之后你会发现它的价
值：青春和健康；但青春逝去，未见的
活力不在、睿智不在、优雅不在。而失
去健康，即使青春犹在，年轻与你何
用，财富与你何用，时间与你何用。地
位与你何用。

Figure 4 Teacher Han's post (used with permission).

reproduction of landscape. Alongside the artwork, Han's post says the following (translated from the Mandarin):

'There are two things you will discover the value of upon losing them: Youth and good health. When youth is gone, your unseen vitality, intelligence, and elegance are lost. And when good health goes, even when youth is still there, what use is it for you? What use is wealth to you, and what use is status for you?'

The text of Han's post is actually a paraphrasing of a well-known hadith (narrated tradition) from the Prophet Muhammad which instructs people to 'make use of five things before the coming of five things'. Among them are 'your good health before sickness overtakes you' and 'your youth before old age'.

The hadith is depicted but not referenced as a hadith tradition, for to do so would likely result in him being censored. Instead, he dresses up the message as a general piece of wisdom and advice, posing as a Master who provides wisdom and guidance to people through his calligraphy. In discussions with me, both Li and Han talked about conjoining spiritual guidance within their calligraphy instruction as consistent with the way they themselves were taught: 'My Master would not just test my writing; he would test my temperament,' Li relates.

I would regard these elisions and deletions are forms of *situated re-entextualisation* which can be understood through the dynamic movement of certain elements of language and discourse into other settings, modes, and frames in a particular and situated moment such as an online post. Further developing the use of the concept already mentioned previously, and drawing further from Silverstein and Urban (1996), Blommaert (2005) refers to the *re-entextualisation* of texts which are subject to a series of transformations in that they become de-contextualised, repackaged, reorganised, and made relevant by (or, in the case of these posts, *for*) another audience. Relatedly, Kell (2015) has termed the study of these processes 'transcontextual analysis'. Despite some variations in terminology, these ideas claim that through various means of re-contextualisation not only is the language of a particular text reconfigured and transformed semiotically, but also, and perhaps more importantly, new meanings and associations created as it travels across space and time. In further work Kell (2017) argues for developed notion of a textual 'meaning-making trajectory' in which, at certain points or 'nodes', texts become reified into something else as part of the flow of meaning making across time and space. With steps in the analytic process, new texts are brought about that become reified both within and beyond a particular audience, where the effects of power relations and communicative norms become evident.

However, my attempt to understand the calligraphers' posts about their work in similar ways requires an acknowledgement that I am not studying any text trajectory per se, as each post is a standalone event though consisting of multifaceted texts and entextualised renditions. Rather, they are what I would prefer to call *situated re-entextualisations* of heritage knowledge. For this, Blommaert's (2005) term 're-entextualisation' reflects more closely the processes and changes manifested in this section of data.

As Blommaert (2005, p. 47) outlines, through re-entextualisation, discourses become 'associated to a new context and accompanied by a particular metadiscourse which provides a sort of "preferred reading" for the [new] discourse'. The language work of the calligraphers is therefore as important as their brushstrokes in each transformation of the text: From already entextualised original calligraphy piece, to redacted and distilled Chinese version beside it, with the further redacted and distilled text of a post. Each stage is purposefully ordered through a set of strategic and gradual moves through the use of particular discursive resources. The elisions by Teachers Li and Han create hidden references to religion in order to avoid being censored on China's heavily monitored and controlled social media. Their posts thus have to become rendered into *something other than themselves*. They must 'tip-toe along the red-lines' (Wang 2019b) and, as I shall describe in more detail herein, engage in forms of *covert semiosis*.

It is almost as if with each re-entextualisation, the previous one need not exist. In only working with the first entextualisation (the hand-crafted work of art), the task is not complete. For Teachers Li and Han, scriptural art requires an exegesis, or commentary of some sort. This is the way. In bygone times this would have been in a lecture as masters taught how to write scriptural art, they also provided exegetical readings for meditation. Now this occurs within a 'postdigital literacy ecology' (see Bhatt 2023a) which integrates performance-based practice, exegetical reading, religious theology, Chinese art, and the platform's sensitive word censorship system. Something is, therefore, likely to be lost in the process, as a new metapragmatic framing necessitates elisions and deletions, leading to comprehensive transformations rather than a replication of an original text. In some ways this is an inevitable part of the *platformisation* of heritage literacy.

Therefore, situated re-entextualisation can be said to occur when entextualised heritage knowledge is transformed through processes such as re-interpretation, re-organisation, and refashioning in a particular and co-present moment of heritage instruction, which is precisely what Teachers Li and Han are considered to be doing for their audience. Importantly, therefore, not every new representation is accessible to everyone, and re-entextualisation practices depend on who has access to either a contextual space, or in this case resources. Clearly, so far, the censoring artificial intelligence system of the Weixin platform has not blocked Teachers Li and Han for religious content, nor the calligraphy student Baojie for her posts. This is likely because Sini Calligraphy is considered a form of national cultural heritage.[23] We could say that 'imagistically' it is allowed, but for textual renditions the calligraphers play things much more carefully. Their followers online are also a mix of people who follow them for different reasons, including committed calligraphy students, general enthusiasts for Islamic and/or Chinese art, and interested people from various non-Muslim communities. The point is that as they post about their work, and as heritage knowledge is re-entextualised, it is also 're-accentuated' (Bakhtin 1984) for their diverse audience. This means that they do not merely reproduce their work for all, but rather that they appropriate the voices (or accents; perceptions) of their audience with new renderings, versions, and purposes.

While heritage knowledge that is re-entextualised in this way may still show traces of the original production, the accompanying posts are clearly re-inscribed

---

[23] See 'Islamic Calligraphy in China', *China Heritage Quarterly* 5 (March 2006), www.chinaher itagequarterly.org/features.php?searchterm=005_calligraphy.inc&issue=005.

with new meanings. This is not simply about making Sini calligraphy easier to understand or more accessible. The re-interpretations of the meanings of the original texts that occur in re-entextualisation involve some quite radical changes. These re-interpretations result from two related interpretative processes: a calligraphy teacher's understandings of the meanings in the original entextua-lised knowledge, and their perceptions of the expectations of their diverse online followers.

Notably, for these Sini calligraphers situated re-entextualisation here is constituted as 'an act of control' (Bauman and Briggs 1990, p. 76) through which they can claim a degree of agency in creating their work, explaining its significance, strategically re-glossing it to avoid censorship, and all the while maintaining the attention of their audience as carriers and purveyors of Sino-Muslim heritage since the time of Liu Zhi.

For people like Teachers Li and Han, practices of re-entextualisation play an important role in the battle over boundaries and in tip-toeing the red-lines of what is deemed acceptable content in Chinese social media. Their examples are analytically important because they demonstrate distinctive discursive strat-egies to legitimise and normalise Sini calligraphy through the recontextualising of their work and its undergirding religious message into a space that must remain secularised.[24] The examples point to attempts by Sino-Muslims to regulate their own digital practices in light of censorship and curbs on religious activity, particularly online. There are numerous examples within the dataset of how Sino-Muslims navigate such red-lines, with users demarcating their social media networks into different audiences (for fear of being misunderstood by non-Muslim compatriots while posting on religion), and often self-censoring and having to figure out which 'sensitive words' resulted in their post being removed or account banned. These are further discussed in Section 4.

In order to examine Sini calligraphy, we need to also look at how words and objects co-constitutively shape meaning and form powerful artefacts of reli-gious heritage. Literacy here has to be looked at as part of lived religion, the religious practice of everyday life rather than as defined by religious organisa-tions or indeed a top-down imposed sense of Hui heritage. To some extent this is already a key commitment within literacy studies (the focus on everyday literacies), but here I wish to emphasise that there are number of binaries that can be disrupted by this commitment with respect to heritage literacy: the binary of religious and secular, of the personal and the private, and institutional and informal – all of which have major implications when examining anything

---

[24] During the period of the research, I became aware of a man from Yunnan Province who was arrested and jailed for two years for teaching people how to pray via the same social media platform.

dubbed as 'religious practice' in China. This commitment also entails looking at how calligraphy's symbolism is manifested by Sino-Muslims, an issue to which I now turn.

The Symbolic Weight of 'Jīng'

Sini calligraphy is essentially about meaning-making and symbolism. As with any art form that originates from writing, its symbolism supersedes its linguistic meaning, and this is why we see its use alongside covert forms of interpretation, and with immense affective attachment as a form of 'intangible cultural heritage' for Sino-Muslims. Its symbolism, however, is attached to its Arabic origins in Quranic scripture and this aspect deserves some further analysis. Therefore, in order to widen the analytical frame for this subsection, I draw from work on 'semiotic ideologies' (Keane 2018), key to which is Keane's definition of the term as 'people's underlying assumptions about what signs are, what functions signs do or do not serve, and what consequences they might or might not produce' (Keane 2018, p. 65). To some extent this concept cuts across all the content of this Element, as the various modalities used in practices of heritage literacy are themselves the result of particular historical circumstances and events which contribute to the ways in which Sino-Muslims use and interpret them, and subsequently, form judgments of spiritual and political value. I therefore must analyse heritage literacy as part of a 'representational economy' (Keane 2007, 2018). That is, whether Sini calligraphy is engaged with aesthetically (as art), hermeneutically (as scripture), or emblematically (as tradition), is dependent on its modes of signification at the level of the *everyday*. This approach has the potential to go beyond a priori notions of what qualifies as 'secular', 'religious', or even specifically 'Chinese' contexts. Semiotic ideology not only takes my analysis beyond the concept of 'language ideology' (Irvine and Gal 2009) by expanding from sets of beliefs and feelings about language and into semiosis more generally, but also into territory wherein the object of signification itself may be in dispute. For example, what would (or not) cause a research participant to count a sign as 'Chinese' or 'Islamic', how would such a claim be mediated, and what would such a sign portend for them?

The previous section has highlighted how, as a confluence of traditions, there is a co-dependency between – and simultaneity of – Arabic and Chinese concepts in Sini calligraphy work. The persistent use of Arabic – even when sinicised – works as a valorised indexical for sacredness. This means that, as a trope, its powerful indexical quality is dependent on the Sino-Muslim valorisation of Arabic as the characteristic language of 'jīng' (经; scripture; classic). The notion of indexicality that I am employing in this context refers to the way in which language and other forms of semiotic practice create significance based on the connection between semiosis and specific ideologies. This phenomenon is commonly studied in the fields of sociolinguistics and linguistic anthropology, as noted by Silverstein (2003) and further developed by Blommaert (2005). How Sino-Muslims respond to sacred calligraphy in everyday literate practice tells us a lot about the relationship between the community's prevalent semiotic ideologies vis-à-vis religious heritage. In order to best understand this indexical relationship, and to see matters of semiotic ideology, we need to look outside of calligraphy and more towards Perso-Arabic features in everyday practices of heritage literacy.

For example, research participants often referred to their conferred Arabic name, which was sometimes used within the family and community, as their 'scripture name' (经名; jīngmíng). Some only used the scripture name at home, and others beyond the home and into the wider Hui community. Others would use it also when they sojourned in Muslim majority countries.[25] Participants often referred to Arabic writing as 'jīngzì' (经字; scripture writing), the study of religion as 'niànjīng' (念经; to read the scripture), and those who study religion as 'niànjīngrén' (念经人; people who read the scripture). Clearly, therefore, scripture, or the concept of jing as a semiotic device, operates as part of a system of signification within a 'representational economy' (cf Keane) that constitutes heritage. Naming oneself and others, people in the community, scripts, language, and much more can all be seen as oriented to jing as part of heritage (broadly defined). However, varying semiotic ideologies will also govern what jing is for individual Sino-Muslims, and how it is to function in their world. In other words, it is the relationship that individual Sino-Muslims have with jing that tells us something about which name they use, and when they choose to use it (including as a form of *covert semiosis*). Examining that relationship becomes a key component of the study, therefore.

An example of a participant's relationship with Perso-Arabic script, despite not knowing how to read it, comes from Meili who was raised in Xinjiang Uighur Autonomous Region. She provided a detailed account of her relationship with Perso-Arabic script and much of this relationship stems from a heritage related connection to its imagery rather than an ability to read it. This is because, unlike participants in previous extracts, her religious learning has not led her to study Arabic. In the following extract, she relays quite an everyday and perhaps slightly embarrassing event at a restaurant in Xinjiang:

---

[25] Semiotic ideologies associated with naming also influenced the pseudonyms given to respondents as the research was reported on; for example, pseudonyms chosen in this Element, be they Chinese, Arabic or English, reflect individual's preferred actual name.

> When I worked in Xinjiang, I thought everything was qingzhen[26] because
> even the toilet room had some Arabic on it. But it turned out that this 'Arabic'
> was actually the Uighur language. After that, I realised that I cannot actually
> tell the difference between Arabic and Uighur!

Meili's experience of mistaking Uighur as Arabic deserves some attention as
her response makes this a matter of semiotic ideology. Uighur is one of China's
minority languages though the Uighur ethnic group is the majority in Xinjiang.
Despite being one of the official languages of the Xinjiang Uighur Autonomous
Region, Mandarin remains the language of upward mobility and economic
advantage. Notably, Uighur adopts a variant of the Perso-Arabic script, so to
the unbeknownst eye they may look the same. Meili's assumption that wherever
such script appears signifies a Muslim presence, and subsequently halal food,
tells us that the Sino-Muslim community's use of Perso-Arabic script brings
with it certain assumptions. Those are assumptions of 'halalness' in many cases
and also more broadly of 'Muslimness' which is over and above food and
consumption practices, though more recent curbs on visible representation of
Arabic in public spaces have impacted the instances when this might readily
occur (see Section 3).

The following is another account which echoes Meili's in terms of the
language ideologies associated with Perso-Arabic script in non-religious settings. Lei is from Xi'an (Shaanxi Province) and studied several years through
the mosque-based scripture hall system and undertook a course of Arabic study
at university. During his university studies, he recalls how his roommate reacted
to his rather unhallowed treatment of an Arabic language text book:

> One day when I was holding an Arabic language text book, my Hui roommate
> said that I was holding 'jing' [scripture], because in his religious conscious-
> ness, Arabic and jing are the same. I'd put the book on the floor or throw it
> about casually, and he would frown at my treatment of Arabic text. I had to
> explain to him that there is a difference between this textbook and actual jing,
> and that I would not treat jing so casually.

Semiotic ideologies surrounding Perso-Arabic script clearly link to how people
feel about the text, the hallowed nature of the script, and the print literacy artefact.
For many Sino-Muslims, Perso-Arabic script has immense *imagistic symbolism*
through its visual representation. Its imagistic presence becomes iconic of something essential about that which it is taken to index, revealing a semiotic ideology
of valorising jing as part of faith. For those who have not experienced the text
outside of heritage spheres, such as Lei's roommate and Meili, seeing the script in

---

[26] See Section 3 for a detailed explanation of this term and its significance in Sino-Muslim heritage
literacy.

a non-religious context such as a bathroom sign or university textbook becomes a moment of important realisation. In their eyes, the bathroom notice and textbook are material objects which are imbued with jing.

How people feel about Arabic words also links closely to decisions about which words to use to describe religious activities. For participants who have networks outside of China, the localised (that is to say, sinicised) and Persian-origin names of everyday forms of worship, had given way to more recently popularised Arabised terms used readily through interactions with the Arab and wider Muslim world. For some, including participant Hechen who is from Qinghai but later moved to Beijing to study and then to the US for work, choosing which terms to use has changed multiple times in his life as he migrated:

> Being educated in Qinghai, I used our localised dialect terms to describe the five daily prayers.[27] During university in Beijing, I was able to meet and interact with other Muslims some of whom were more educated in Arabic, so I ended up 'Arabising' elements of my religious language. Later in life, I missed my roots have now gone back to the localised forms of pronunciation.

Hechen's practices and semiotic ideologies shifted from sinicised Persian-origin words to Arabic due to his expanding religious social sphere, but then back to Sino-acceptance over time. Similar accounts were provided by Sino-Muslim participants in the Ningxia Hui Autonomous Region. One of them is Jinbao, a man in his thirties who undertook a traditional course of religious learning in his childhood and who very rarely travels outside of the province. Here he outlines how, when talking about religious matters, the words he chooses are shaped by various factors:

> To talk about prayer, we use the Mandarin word 'libai' (礼拜) rather than 'namaz'[28] when talking to non-Hui Muslims in China. I use namaz with my family. These terms like namaz, they are our local language of the scripture hall system.
>
> The word 'wudhu'[29] in Mandarin is 'xiaojing' (小净). But we Ningxia Muslims tend to say 'abudaizi' (阿布代兹) which is from the Persian 'abdest'[30] meaning wudhu. My foreign Muslim friends did not understand

---

[27] Hechen's terms for Islam's five daily prayers are derived from Persian but for Qinghai Sino-Muslims form part of a local 'dialect', as follows: 邦达 (bāngdá – dawn prayer; Ar. fajr); 撇什尼 (piēshénní – afternoon prayer; Ar. dhuhur); 底格热 (dǐgérè – late afternoon prayer; Ar. Asr); 沙目 (shāmù – sunset prayer; Ar. Maghrib); 胡夫滩 (húfūtān – night prayer; Ar. Isha).

[28] A common Persian-origin word for prayer (Ar. salah) which in Chinese is sometimes rendered as '乃麻子'.

[29] Islamic ritual water cleansing.

[30] See Wang (2001) for a detailed glossary of Chinese Islamic terms. Most entries within the volume originate from Persian and Arabic, and Wang usefully provides the Semitic transcription alongside each entry.

me and I had to show them what I meant through postures and gestures. After that, I realised that 'abudaizi' means wudhu. I learn from them.

Jinbao's account tells us something about the linguistic choices Sino-Muslims like him make when talking about heritage and religious practice with people outside of China. The Hui are the largest Muslim minority in China, and for the other Chinese Muslim minorities he will use the Mandarin word 'libai' when talking about salah. On the other hand, conversing with foreign Muslims allows for moments of learning in order to expand his, and likely their, vocabulary. Notice how the initial word used, 'abudaizi', was not understood by his interlocutors which caused him to have to demonstrate the act of water cleansing (wudhu) for them to recognise it. Here the bodily performance is the original sign, the essential quality, or sacred idiom, upon which their mutual semiotic ideologies converge. For a brief moment, languages which emerged through their respective nationalistic ideologies were put aside in favour of the transnational idiom of religious gesture and performance.

Jia, another Ningxia participant, has a slightly different approach and set of attitudes to Jinbao. Jia did not have a childhood religious education and was not exposed to a lot of Arabic in her life.

> We Hui have some Hui terms for things which are unknown to Han. When we use them, they won't understand. This is good that we have these. For example, when we greet each other, we say 'bi si mi lia', though actually I don't have special feelings for Arabic, because I seldom see or use it in my life. I think I prefer to use terms like 'Kaizhai' (开斋) than 'Erde' (尔德),[31] as I don't hear people saying Erde so often.

In the extract Jia mixes up the Muslim greeting 'salam' (in Mandarin sometimes rendered as 赛俩目) with the expression 'bismallah' ('In The Name Of God') said for grace, and then explains how she has no 'special feelings' for Arabic due to a lack of opportunities to use Arabesque terms for religious acts and events. Like others in the research, this reveals how heritage practices place Sino-Muslims within a liminal linguistic space between the wider Muslim world on the one hand and Chinese society on the other. For Sino-Muslims like Hechen and Jinbao, 'Arabising' of religious language serves as an important unifier which connects them to co-religionists in the broader Muslim world. It allows them to identify with all Muslims by the preservation of Arabic language elements of the religious tradition and its idiom of performance, despite its branching into multiple culturally inflected sub-traditions far removed from Islam's place of origin. On the other hand, Jia, like many Sino-Muslims, cares much less about

---

[31] The sinicised form of Arabic word Eid (the Islamic religious festival).

paying homage to Arabic terms. 'Going back' to localised forms or 'Hui terms'
when it comes to defining religious rituals is not so straightforward either. First, it
has as much to do with the specificities of communicative encounters (audience,
etc.) as it has with a reinvigoration of their Chineseness as Sino-Muslims.
Furthermore, many local 'dialect' features of religious terms are often of
Arabic or Persian origin and these can be set apart from their regular Mandarin
equivalents. There are, therefore, multiple decisions to make about language at
the everyday level.[32]

I would argue that tensions around semiotic ideologies among Sino-Muslims
today relate to the search for a divine nomenclature in Sino-Muslim historical
heritage. The issue even emerges with respect to how Sino-Muslims have talked
about God over the centuries. Some Sino-Muslim scholars argue that Chinese
Muslims should preserve within their discursive tradition, as closely as possible, the original Semitic epithet for the monotheistic 'Allāh', thereby asserting
the importance of the Arabic heritage that all Muslims are connected to and
must sustain. Sini calligraphy is one way that this bond is maintained, at least
visually. Many Muslims agree that this divine name defies all translation and
therefore cannot be substituted. It was thus rendered into a transliterated form of
'Ānlā' (安拉) in some Sino-Muslim historical works (see Petersen 2018,
pp. 151–2). As Raphael Israeli argues, in Chinese 'there has hardly been
a conclusively and universally accepted rendering of the monotheistic God'
(Israeli 1997, in Frankel 2011, p. 159). Nevertheless there is a precedent for
non-Arab Muslims to adopt localised substitute names in addition to Allāh,[33]
for example 'khuda' used in Urdu. Muslim, Christian, and Jewish writers trying
express their religious ideas in Chinese have thus experimented with various
words over the centuries. In a detailed discussion on this issue, Frankel (2011),
in his work *Rectifying God's Name*, argues that

> The imperative to find a Chinese name for Allah drew Muslim writers to
> embrace the term that has never held currency in the language of Chinese
> religio-philosophical discourse, but which has been used extensively by
> monotheists in China, namely *zhu*, or 'lord'.[34] (Frankel 2011, p. 160)

---

[32] In 1991 the American anthropologist Dru Gladney compiled a selected glossary of Hui Chinese
Islamic terms as addendum to his book *Muslim Chinese: Ethnic Nationalism in the People's
Republic* (see Gladney 1991). Unlike Wang's (2001) volume, Gladney's entries are entirely
sinicised words; that is to say, they are mostly words which have entered Chinese Islam through
Taoism, Confucianism, etc.

[33] The precedent comes directly from the Islamic tradition: 'whichever you call, He has the Most
Beautiful Names' (Quran 17:110, translation by Pikthall).

[34] This then became the compound 'Zhēnzhǔ' (真主; Eng. True Lord) used by all Abrahamic
monotheists in China, but later used only by Sino-Muslims, as the ancient Chinese deity Shangdi
became equated with the Christian Lord of Heaven (see Frankel 2011, p. 174). Practically all the
participants in the study used the term 'zhenzhu'.

Building on arguments from Israeli (1997), Frankel (2011) further contends that

> Muslims opted for this term precisely because it is not frequently used in Chinese religion and as a means of 'differentiation from the Chinese religious terms (Buddhist and Daoist) lest of the Believers, or the uninformed non-believers, might find too much of a terminological rapprochement between them and Islam.' (Frankel 2011, p. 160)

This tells us that how Sino-Muslims talk about God is something to observe in everyday practice and open to variation in different contexts, just as Hechen would talk about prayer. While most of the research participants use the sinicised 'Zhēnzhǔ' (真主; True Lord), rather than the transliterated 'Ānlā' which appears occasionally in Sino-Muslim literature, there still remain Sino-Muslims who refuse to use Zhenzhu and prefer Anla since the latter is derived from Arabic. Others, however, disapproved of the transliterated Anla since in Chinese pronunciation it omits the last Arabic letter (ء; haa') and adds the 'n' at the end of the first syllable.

Therefore, Arabic (and to a lesser extent Persian) occupies a highly affective and indexical role in the lives of Sino-Muslims, even if it is via imagistic and metalinguistic qualities rather than through an ability to read or communicative competence. In other words, in quotidian communications they connote Muslimness rather than being foreign words which carry linguistic meaning. This kind of symbolic quality has been termed 'postvernacularity' by Shandler (2006). Writing about the role of a language within a cultural group who largely do not use the language in an everyday sense, or after it ceases to function as a spoken language, Shandler's analysis concerned the symbolic value invested in semiotic objects (in our case Perso-Arabic forms) leading to their status as language items which exist in 'several imaginary worlds' and characterised by 'geographical otherness'. For Shandler (2006), postvernacularity emerges in the 'self-conscious, contingent, and tenacious' (p. 20) linguistic practices of group members. The symbolic values invested in Sini calligraphy (as a form of heritage literacy) have expanded greatly and have done so because of a prevailing sense that new cultural possibilities for heritage literacy must be tenaciously sought out in the quest for meta-meaning.

Through Sini calligraphy, Sino-Muslims are reminded of the deep symbolism and religious importance of the Arabic language as the language of jing. Its postvernacularity entails that its symbolic value precedes and supersedes any ability to understand it, as was the case with Meili and Lei's college roommate. Lack of fluency does not impede one's attempt to pay homage to the language for religious purposes, assuming its metalinguistic quality is acknowledged as a sign of Muslimness. As we have seen with Meili, this can even be when language is mistakenly identified as jing. In the next sections we attempt to investigate further how such indexical connections manifest using data from public signage.

3 The Semiotics of Food Heritage

Sino-Muslim Food Heritage

This section turns to the semiotic material of restaurant signage and food packaging, as part of a broader understanding of food heritage in the Sino-Muslim community. It begins with an account of shop signage at a location known as 'Huiminjie' (回民街; commonly referred to as 'Muslim Street'), a Sino-Muslim cultural hub within the city of Xi'an (Shaanxi Province). I will also utilise data from two other similar locations: the Chengdong District of Xining (Qinghai Province) and Litong in Wuzhong (Ningxia Province). These are two areas that have undergone investments in the tourism sector, which has resulted in a revalorising and revitalising of Sino-Muslim food heritage based on a spirit of ethnic entrepreneurialism. Through mostly image-based data obtained from linguistic landscaping and supplementary interviews with participants (including food vendors), I examine how signage relies on indexical connections between the Arabic language, and other Sino-Muslim heritage markers in the public space. Later in the section, I also draw from various forms of food packaging from Sino-Muslim brands.

In considering the role food plays in representing and preserving Sino-Muslim heritage, it is important to understand how religious rituals are often configured around food. These include the two Eids, weddings and 'nietie'[35] (乜贴; events of voluntary alms giving). Memories are thus inscribed, consciously or unconsciously, in food consumption, and food itself becomes an effective tool for heritage maintenance. But food also serves to differentiate (Greco 2022) and becomes central to identity work, orientations to 'groupness', and the existence of external 'others'. For Sino-Muslims, buying qingzhen food products and eating at qingzhen restaurants is not just an act of religious observation but a means of differentiating themselves from the majority Han population (the external other). In China, Muslim dietary prohibitions are often a barrier in social and professional situations where meetings and events will take place around food and alcohol. A participant, whose father is Han Chinese, recalled eating at her father's family home as follows:

---

[35] This is actually a transliteration of the Arabic word 'niyya' (intention) and in Sino-Muslim contexts has come to relate to any act of giving, including in more formalised ways at particular lifecycle events and commemorations (e.g. the Prophet's birth, weddings, marriages).

> When we go to my father's family home, we use our own bowls and cutlery.
> Because they are 'Hanmin' [Han people], I do not eat the food they prepared,
> I eat instant noodles at the table with them, or eat outside before I arrive there.

Since a person 'gives off' something about themselves through their culinary choices, those actions become decidedly semiotic acts and salient to my study. Qingzhen food has become an integral part of Sino-Muslim heritage, consumption patterns, ethnic place-making, and a site for where identity-related semiotic practices take place. It is for this reason that the qingzhen food industry is leveraged by the state, as argued by Stroup (2022) in his ethnographic study of Sino-Muslims in Qinghai Province:

> [T]he Chinese state seeks to promote and control the qingzhen food industry in
> order to showcase ethnic diversity and celebrate displays of ethnic differenti-
> ation that accord with its narrative of ethnic unity. Doing so allows the state to
> cast the development of the halal food industry as yet another benchmark in the
> state's quest for inclusivity and progress. (Stroup 2022, p. 98)

This section therefore aims to explore how Sino-Muslim cultural identity is expressed and negotiated through different semiotic practices as part of food heritage activity, and how hybridities (commercial-religious and ethnic-national, among others) generate tensions and peculiarities between diversity, integration, and place-making. In this respect, it is necessary to consider not just food culture and consumption, but more generally how Sino-Muslim religio-cultural identity is expressed, constructed, and remembered through them, and the semiotic role of materiality in this regard.

The Mosque and the Marketplace

Huiminjie, also known as 'Muslim Street' or 'the Muslim Quarter' (see Figure 5), in the city of Xi'an is a vibrant and culturally important area known for its array of Muslim businesses, tourism, mosques, and financial activity. Muslim Street is home to a variety of businesses, including halal restaurants, clothing shops and a souvenir market. It is also a popular destination for tourists, who come to explore the area's rich cultural heritage, visit the tangentially located mosques and Islamic cultural sites, and sample the local qingzhen cuisine. Local iconic products include beef balls (牛肉丸; niúròu wán), crispy beef (小酥肉; xiǎosūròu), and eight-treasure steamed rice (八宝蒸饭; bābǎo zhēngfàn).

The area also plays an important role in the city's cultural and religious life, as it is home to several historic mosques and Islamic cultural institutions, such as the Great Mosque of Xi'an (Figure 2). The quarter covers several blocks (around 500 metres long), and is inhabited by over 20,000 Sino-Muslims, many of whom are purported to be descendants of Muslim merchants and diplomatic envoys who

Figure 5 Huiminjie ('Muslim Street'), Xi'an (photo by Nuhha).

settled in the area. Given its location, the origin story of Muslim Street is an important factor in terms of its food heritage authenticity. In a well-cited ethnographic study on life in Xi'an's Muslim Quarter, Maris Gillette (2000) recalls how the physical boundaries of the quarter were ambiguous. Despite the lack of official demarcations, Gillette found that Sino-Muslim residents were able to identify the cultural (and hence geographic) boundaries of their quarter (Gillette 2000, p. 31). Living in close proximity to fellow community members also provided a sense of belonging and practical benefits to those who called this neighbourhood home. As an urban enclave, Muslim Street became a crucial site for preserving Sino-Muslim cultural traditions and sustaining connections to heritage (Gillette 2000).

This study was conducted over two decades after Gillette's, yet locally based participants echoed similar sentiments about Muslim Street's lack of officially recognised borders. Local interviewees described it as being largely 'self-built' but nonetheless with cultural and geographic boundaries that are intuitively decipherable by locals. Proximity to places of worship and fellow believers create the conditions for effective preservation of cultural traditions and sustaining connections to ethnic identity. This is made further relevant by the closeness in relations between the mosque and the marketplace. Comparable Sino-Muslim enclaves in China's major cities are also often located near or around mosques, including Xining's Chengdong District, where vendors sell qingzhen food, and other religious products in streets adjoining the famous Dongguan Mosque.

The relationship local residents have with Muslim Street is slightly complicated. For example, Yating, a food vendor and long-time resident whom I met and interacted extensively with, recalls an ambivalence towards the quarter alongside the complexity of her expressions of local attachment:

> I love and hate Muslim Street. My work has a lot to do with this area, but I especially hate this place, because the environment I grew up and now work in could be best described as a slum. That is, there is no heating and no natural gas; there is also its litter, the chaos of self-built houses, the quality of staff is unreliable, and it is hard for the government to manage the area; and the road traffic causes narrow, dirty, and messy streets. So, I definitely have a love-hate relationship with this place.

It is important to highlight that during the period immediately prior to this fieldwork, all the Arabic signage in Xi'an's Muslim Street, the Chengdong District of Xining, and in Litong had been removed as part of a drive to 'sinicise' all public spaces. These changes did not occur as a gradually implemented policy, but as an abrupt policy-driven cultural diktat which affected the social environment, the morale of vendors, and the area's image locally. This was despite an otherwise 'hands-off' approach to governance in other aspects, as Yating outlines. Sino-Muslim shop keepers and vendors were left with no choice but to tear down all Arabic words and phrases on their shop signs (often with traces remaining, as we shall come to see) and replace them with terms represented by Chinese characters only. This, however, does not prevent the signage from being important to my analysis of it as part of the study of heritage literacy, and particularly in my attempt to explore forms of covert semiosis. The cooking and serving of some of China's best cuisine remains a notable feature of China's Muslim communities and one particular area where elements of heritage can emerge publicly despite curbs on how it is allowed to appear and be described. For example, in Figure 6 we can see the following depicted: 'Food for people in Huifang [Hui community] and his/her ["TA"] friends', with the characters for qingzhen (清真) on the left.

If one looks carefully, one can also see the remnants of the scraped off 'halal' sign in Arabic (حلال) above the Chinese qingzhen (清真) which replaced it. Changing the script or term for halal does not in any way effect the 'halalness' of the food being made and served but here what is interesting is that the Arabic text is still partly visible and within imagistic grasp. During the research, I noticed that almost all shop signs had halal signs either scraped off, covered

Figure 6 Halal eatery called 'Mu Ba La Ke' (photo by author).

by tape, or painted over. This observation raises several questions regarding the intention behind imposing language restrictions on Arabic in public spaces. We have seen in the previous section on Sini calligraphy how Sini-Arabesque writing (and we can include signage here) has usually bespoken a localised sense of Muslimness. However, current state policy views all Arabic signage (both standard and in many cases Sini styles) as denoting 'a spectral threat of transnational Islam' (Ha 2020, p. 427). At its root perhaps is the underlying sense that Arabic script can position Sino-Muslims as the 'foreign other' to Han viewers of the signs, and simultaneously be perceived as a way that Sino-Muslim themselves exclude, and thereby create a sense of 'otherness', for the Han Chinese. Viewed either way, it is clearly a differentiating device.

Data show that such language curbs vary across different parts of China (see Figure 12 taken in Shanghai, for example) and can even impact verbal inter-action in areas where it has applied in its most severe form, as Ping from Shandong Province informs:

> When I was on holiday in Kashgar [in Xinjiang Uighur Autonomous Region], we went to eat at a restaurant. I kept asking the staff if the food is qingzhen, and they never answered me. Just ignored me. Our tour guide took me to the side and cautioned me from using religious words in public, and to just assume that it is qingzhen because 'everything is qingzhen here in Kashgar'.[36]

The rather bizarre refrain from uttering religious words in a public space bespeaks a climate of religious sensitivity, censorship, and language policing

---

[36] For a more detailed account of the history of religious culture in Xinjiang Uighur Autonomous Region and its connections with the recent sinicisation agenda see Thum (2018).

that occurs between citizens. The tour guide's assumption that it must be qingzhen because 'everything is qingzhen here' is an assumption also reflected in Muslim Street and tells us something about the semiotic power of the term in place-making in Chinese-Muslim enclaves. This is the case even when religious words are not visible or utterable. Yating tells of how her mother would never check if a food store in Muslim Street was qingzhen (signage or not), but when she travels outside of the area she makes a point of asking to check before purchasing food items. However, the term 'qingzhen' suggests much more than its metonymic equivalent 'halal'.

According to different sources, the term 'qingzhen' comes from Taoism or Buddhism, and means 'pure and true'. An early use of the term was by the famous Tang era poet Li Bai (d. 762AD).[37] It was purportedly used by the founding Ming emperor Zhu Yuanzhang, also in a poem,[38] to refer to Islam as 'the religion called the Pure and True' (教名清真; jiào míng qīngzhēn; see Ma and Newlon 2022). It is also reflected in the word for mosque as 'pure and true temple' (清真寺; qīngzhēnsì). The word is thus a marker of Chinese Islamic indigenousness, and goes beyond the Arabic term halal which commonly signifies dietary prescription and means 'permitted' (i.e. in Sacred Law). It also differs from the Arabic word in its historical trajectory, ideational connotations,[39] and, crucially in light of current policies, its political implications (see Ha 2020 for an account of these differences).

The argument that qingzhen is deployed as a linguistic device indexical of heritage beyond mere ritual slaughter and consumption practice is consistent with an account given by Yating, a Sino-Muslim food vendor in Xi'an. Yating describes the connection that qingzhen food has with her ethno-religious identity, business choices, and Islamic rituals in the following ways:

> Qingzhen is firstly a sign of the difference in food consumption between the Hui and Han nationalities. We must first distinguish the difference between us and other ethnic groups with respect to food: Qingzhen food. I use it in my mind to divide the standard of what I can eat and what I cannot eat. It is a benchmark.

And in terms of her approach to her heritage food and ritual, she says:

---

[37] Li Bai's couplet from 'Gufeng daya jiubuzuo' (古风·大雅久不作) is as follows: '聖代復元古, 垂衣貴清真'. Translated as 'The Great Dynasty (Tang) is returning to the policies of ancient dynasties that aimed to not take any actions against the pure and true' (Li Bai 1935, p. 90).

[38] The poem is called 'baizizan' (百字赞; One Hundred Words of Praise) and its couplets laud Islam and praise the Prophet Muhammad.

[39] The way in which qingzhen has been conceptualised through the data could very easily equate to the Quranic terms 'halal and tayyib' (Quran 2:168) in which the word 'tayyib' (pure/good) is paired with halal.

We will cleanse our bodies[40] before cooking, considering it an act of worship. This is common in our community.

While attachments to food heritage in Muslim Street may not always remain constant, they can evolve with shifting attitudes over time, and reflect the enduring connection to qingzhen cuisine. Though not everyone in Muslim Street is as meticulous as Yating in this regard:

> Things are becoming more and more different. After the new generation's growth, more and more post-90s and post-00s Hui are now getting married differently. Hui parents may find it more troublesome to do a traditional wedding with the usual dishes, and so to a large extent they will simplify the wedding. After simplifying the wedding, there is no difference from the Han nationality's wedding. There is increasingly less culture to pass on.

In this respect the term 'qingzhen' represents a set of ethics over and above ritual requirements with food. Its connection in this context with place-making, ritual, and inheritance becomes most stark in the Muslim holy month of Ramadhan. Muslim Street in the month of Ramadhan highlights the impermeable bond between cuisine and spirituality as a quintessential instance of ritualistic production and consumption that is firmly rooted in a specific context. The collective observance of the breaking of the fast unites individuals across temporal and spatial boundaries through discourses of heritage and religion. For Sino-Muslims, food, like other forms of heritage, evokes a sense of tradition that must be safeguarded in the face of rapid change that challenges the identity of communities. As a result, qingzhen food, as heritage cuisine, is a semiotically powerful means to preserve identity by distinguishing itself from new and globally ubiquitous foods sold elsewhere, even if it means using new and innovative means to re-package tradition. Sino-Muslims thus use the trope of qingzhen as a way to balance the tensions between conservatism, as manifested in cultural memory, and capitalism, with the promotion of novel customs alongside adherence to traditional practices.

The sign in Figure 7 is from a restaurant which was newly opened at the time of the research and located in a city within the Northeast region of China. The sign which contains the phrase 'Islamic Food' and 'China & Halal' was prominently placed on all the exterior and interior walls of the premises, as well as on every menu, table, and even every cutlery holder. The extensive displays served to continuously and explicitly remind customers that the restaurant serves 'Islamic food'. Perhaps this is to exploit the permissibility of using an English sign when an Arabic one is not allowed? Some other

---

[40] Referring to Islamic ritual water cleansing (Ar. wudhu; Ch. 小净; xiǎojìng).

Figure 7 A restaurant sign in a city within the Northeast of China
(photo by author).

restaurants, including in Northwestern cities where language curbs are most intense, even went by English names like 'Muslim Food' or 'Muslim Restaurant'. When I had the opportunity to ask the owners, I found that they had used the term 'qingzhen' interchangeably with the English terms 'Muslim' and 'Islamic'. In some of these cases, signs depicting the Arabic equivalent of 'Islamic restaurant' (المطعم الاسلامي; *al mat'am al islami*) had been removed and 'Northwestern' used in its place, as shown in Figure 8 taken in Hangzhou (Zhejiang).

There were dozens of examples of the ghostly presence of partially removed or partially covered Arabic text on shop signs across all cities where the language curbs had been applied. In Figure 9, taken in Xining, we can see the visible traces of the fixings that held the letters, exposing the complete length of the Arabic text that previously adorned the restaurant's facade. As with many other similar cases observed (including as in Figure 8), Arabic is clearly still discernible, but now stands as a remnant of a prior text juxtaposed with the newly added category equivalents that were sought in the revised sign.

Beyond signage, not everyone is careful in observing qingzhen ethics when it comes to food and business choices. There were some, albeit very few, in the research who owned establishments that were not even registered as qingzhen. For example, Xing runs a coffee shop in Litong with his cousins who are also Sino-Muslims. But he has not registered the coffee shop as qingzhen even though it serves food:

> The qingzhen label requires procedures and our coffee shop has not yet applied for it. It is not like I intentionally avoid mentioning [i.e. in the sign] that our coffee shop is qingzhen, it's just that people here don't care.

Figure 8 Arabic for 'Islamic restaurant' (المطعم الاسلامي; al mat'am al islami) has been removed and 'Northwestern People' used in its place in Hangzhou (photo by author).

Figure 9 The visible traces of the fixings that once held the Arabic sign in place across a restaurant's façade in Xining (photo by author).

For Xing, the main obstacle is the application and set of procedures that he must undertake in order to become an officially recognised qingzhen business. In looking into the procedure for a 'halal permit' (清真许可证; qīngzhēn xǔkě zhèng), Zichao, a participant who works for one of the halal certification authorities told me that

> Across China it depends on which department of the local government is in charge of this matter; either Ethnic and Religious Affairs Commission, Religious Affairs Bureau, or Administrative Approval Bureau ... The two-character qingzhen (清真) is found in most of China, including Shaanxi, except

in Ningxia where it should be 'qingzhen shipin' (清真食品; qingzhen food).
but no such labelling is allowed in Xinjiang. In Xinjiang, you cannot have any
sign or labels saying 'qingzhen'.

It is unclear why the precise wording and presentation style of qingzhen labels
varies across different provinces, though the outright ban on even using the
sinicised term in Xinjiang echoes the experience of Ping from Shandong
Province mentioned earlier. Formalised processes contrast with another account
of qingzhen branding as a form of religious endorsement that is more localised
and via religious figures, as Kaiye relates:

> Some people will open a restaurant and invite a local Ahong to make a prayer
> (Ar. *dua*) at the premises as it opens. Then, everyone in the community will
> know it is qingzhen.

The discourse of qingzheng is therefore one that is rooted in, and constitutive of,
multiple semiotic ideologies. One is from the perspective of lawmakers and
certifiers like Zichao whose job it is to check premises and rather dispassion-
ately issue a certificate. The other, as related by Kaiye, is from a local Ahong
who, at the behest of new owners, prays (i.e. offers 'dua') at the premises as it
opens in front of others so Sino-Muslim locals know it is Muslim-owned and
thus qingzhen. One process is rather official and legalistic, and can even be for
purposes of branding and tourism, and the other is very much unofficial and
community situated. Yet both are concerned with the perceived 'Muslimness' of
the restaurant. Each uses a semiotic ideology that engages with Sino-Muslim
food heritage in different ways. In the more unofficial process, sometimes the
physical branding may not even be sought after, in which case the act of
signification is imputed as restaurants rely on their local reputation for being
qingzhen. As we saw with Yating's mother, who doesn't bother checking local
restaurants if they are qingzhen but does when she is in other areas of the city,
this may have a lot to do with where a restaurant is located.

   Both kinds of semiotic ideology pertaining to qingzhen apply to Yating, who,
as we have seen already, is very attached to qingzhen ethics in both her personal
and business life. Since the pandemic, her business had to shift to a wholly
online presence. She was trying to get her retail unit back at the time of the data
collection, and had been promoting the dishes online through her Weixin
account and 'Meituan', a platform for locally found consumer products and
delivery services. In Figure 10 we can see an image of her handmade gift bags
loaded on the back of a truck ready for delivery to local residents. Through her
online account she also promotes video clips of the food being prepared to
demonstrate its authenticity as qingzhen and native to Muslim Street. Some of
the gift bags are for Han Chinese non-Muslim customers who will distribute

Figure 10 Yating's handmade gift bags loaded on a truck and ready
for delivery (photo by Heng).

them as part of the Chinese New Year. They too seek an authentic qingzheng gift bag, but for branding purposes and the allure of 'Muslim food' – reasons markedly different to her Hui customers. Such is the semiotic power of qingzhen branded food.

Going back to Figure 6, perhaps more tellingly for our purposes, the word 'mubalake' (穆巴拉克) in the sign is not a group of Chinese words at all; it actually equates to one singular word 'mubarak' (lit. 'blessed'), a global Islamic word which originates from Arabic and popular throughout Persia and Asia, but depicted in the sign through Chinese characters. Here we see translingual aspects to heritage literacy and repertoire-based messaging to index something far beyond China and deep into a wider Islamo-sociolinguistic world. It is unlikely that many Han Chinese would know what mubalake means[41] and would consider it as one of many elements of the Hui community's localised dialect, sometimes referred to locally as 'Fangshang Hui' (坊上回) and, thereby, a very different kind of Muslimness. This dialect is a mixture of northern Chinese dialects with embedded Perso-Arabic elements, such as word like mubalake. It has a long history of development and is considered intrinsic to authenticity of local identity (see Bucholtz and Hall 2005). According to a study by Dong (2020), outside of the Muslim Street quarter Sino-Muslims will likely use the Xi'an dialect and,

---

[41] Suffice to say that when I first saw this sign and the word 'mubalake', being familiar with South Asian Islamic terminology I immediately knew what it meant; however, during a linguistics lecture I delivered at a Chinese university my mostly Han Chinese students did not.

when farther afield, Mandarin Chinese when it comes to interactions with the local Han community.

The function of the mubalake sign, as an artefact of heritage literacy, is that it is *emblematic* as a manifestation of postvernacularity (Shandler 2006; see Section 1). On the one hand, the official language is deployed through recognisable Chinese characters graphically displayed, but also bearing connections with another, and rather distant, language of religious heritage (the Perso-Arabic term 'mubarak'). The sign is not at all motivated by its linguistic meaning, as the four characters 'mu ba la ke' could amount to being meaningless to Han Mandarin speakers, neither does it suggest much about the Perso-Arabic fluency of the authors (the word 'mubarak' is used across Asia by non-Arabs). Instead, it is laden with heritage and religious sentiments which makes it a powerful *indexical* that can serve as a seed for heritage literacy maintenance in a site where Arabesque signage has been purged from public view. By using the term 'indexical' here, I am referring to how the character combination mubalake is designed to signal something in the social world that is understood in different ways. As Blommaert (2005) makes clear, semiotic choices such as these are 'nested in particular *orders of indexicality*' (p. 69). He further argues that 'when people move through physical and social space (both are usually intertwined), they move through orders of indexicality affecting their ability to deploy communicative resources' (p. 69).

Blommaert (2015) further emphasises that a sign can serve different purposes in any given communicative environment where it has been deployed. Its effects will thus depend on how those who engage with it understand its function. Proficiency with Perso-Arabic text could be considered the utmost form of a Sino-Muslim's embodiment of such indexicals, though increasingly rare to see in public in light of current curbs.[42] In lieu of this, taking maximal advantage of what is permitted in the public realm by covert semiosis becomes a necessary tactic.

In Figure 11 we see a small eatery belonging to 'Yīsīhā' (伊斯哈) which is a sinicised rendition of the Arabic for Isaac (إسحاق; pronounced 'ishaq'). Isaac is the name of a Prophet mentioned in the Quran and the Bible and, here, is the vendor's scripture name. Following the name Yīsīhā' is a brief list of the local dishes on offer, including one type of stuffed fried bread for nietie (Islamic alms giving) events. Participants throughout the project described their Islamic name as their 'scripture name' and would usually use it only in specific heritage-related contexts. Other scripture names noted on shop signs included ālǐ (阿里; Ali), mùhǎnmòdé (穆罕默德; Mohammed), and hàshimù (哈什目; Hashim).

---

[42] Throughout the research I inquired about the role of Arabic and Persian in other domains and there seem to be indications of an increase in their uptake for foreign language study in universities (see: www.chinadaily.com.cn/china/2016-01-25/content_23229251.htm).

Figure 11 Yisiha's (Isaac's) halal eatery (photo by author).

The Chinese characters that were used for Arabic scripture names were not standardised across different locations observed.

Another example (see Figure 12) I saw in both Xi'an and Xining, and one which is set apart from the others, is a sign with the name ěrsà (尔萨) which is the sinicised rendition of the Arabic name for Jesus (عيسى; pronounced 'Eissa'). Figure 12 shows a shop selling fresh chicken belonging to someone called ěrsà (尔萨; Ar. Eissa). The sign also contains the Qinghai-specific halal sign at the top right. Eissa is a common name in Muslim communities and is also referenced in the Quranic text some twenty-five times.

I discussed earlier in Section 2 how the divine epithet Zhenzhu (Allāh) was initially used by all three Abrahamic faiths in China, but only remained in use by Sino-Muslims (see Frankel 2011). Similarly, ěrsà (尔萨), as a sinicised epithet for Jesus/Eissa, is not the equivalent one used by contemporary Chinese Christians. The word for Jesus that is usually used by Chinese Christians is yēsū (耶稣), which is transliterated from Latin and not usually used as a person's name. There is therefore diversity in how religious names are used and what written form they take, pointing to the importance of regionality and dialect.

Regionality and place-making are also central to the literacy practices that shape cuisine and culinary work, as Yating reported:

> Muslim Street embodies a kind of regionality. Knowing our area through our food, understanding the life of an area and its culture. Our community's products are iconic and all local to us.

One can contrast the previous images in Xi'an and Xining with Figure 13 which is taken from the semi-open facade of a Sino-Muslim restaurant in the Pudong

Figure 12 A shop selling fresh chicken which has the name ěrsà [尔萨; Ar. Eissa], with the Qinghai halal sign at the top right (photo by author).

Figure 13 Inside a Muslim-owned restaurant in the Pudong District of Shanghai (photo by author).

District of Shanghai. In Figure 13 we can see a large display with various extracts from the Quran, including elements of the 'Fatiha' (the Quran's open-ing chapter), the *Basmala*,[43] and the declaration of faith[44] all depicted in the characteristic Sini style of Arabic. Some parts of the Arabic display are set alongside approximate Chinese translations. The owner of the restaurant told me that he had the artwork commissioned from specialist Quranic engravers in

---

[43] The *Basmala* (or *Tasmiyyah*) is the titular name of the Islamic invocation 'bi-smi llāh' (بِسْمِ ٱللّٰهِ) which translates into 'In the name of Allāh'. The full expression is 'In the name of Allāh, the Most Gracious, the Most Merciful'.

[44] The declaration is known as the 'shahada' and reads 'There is none worthy of worship except God and Muhammad is His messenger'. It is also named by Sino-Muslims as the 'qingzhen yan' (Words of Purity and Truth).

Xi'an and that, through it, he wanted to bring 'the atmosphere of the Northwest' into the diverse Shanghai metropolis. The censorship regulations and curbs on Arabic writing in public spaces in the provinces of Ningxia, Qinghai, and Shaanxi, and more aggressively in Xinjiang, are not (yet) in effect here in the cosmopolitan city of Shanghai. In provinces which have borne the brunt of the curbs on religious symbols in the public sphere, such a partially open exhibit might be unheard of.

The shop signs above all rely on various indexical connections between Perso-Arabic language items and Sino-Muslim heritage and community place-making. Shop signage is a site of contestation in negotiating the boundaries between the sacred and the profane in delineating the boundaries of sociolinguistic difference. They thus offer two kinds of 'meaning effects' (Blommaert 2015, p. 15). The first of these is *denotational*, in that they rely on the conventional and agreed-upon uses of language across communities that operate under a national lingua franca such as Mandarin. This form of meaning is usually static. The second is indexical, and rooted in a specific sub-community's sociocultural and historical body of knowledge. The latter is a more subjective and 'covert' semiosis and intimately tied to heritage literacy practices which occur under the aegis of *shaoshu minzu* (minority ethnic) place-making and consumer practices. But at the same time, they boast a lineage and trajectory which far surpasses this. They are language practices which draw on affective, historical, geographical, and heritage-related attachments and the adaptations of them in signage are ongoing searches for denotational registers. The materialising of Sino-Muslim heritage in this way is a way for those with limited access to heritage literacy, and who may also lack proficiency in Perso-Arabic, to maintain a connection to Islam and the Hui community through food commerce.

The examples draw on the interconnections of Arabic and Perso-Arabic to Sino-Muslim heritage despite the recent removal of Arabic script in signage. The term 'qingzhen' metonymically stands for 'halal' and anything related to Islam. Putting things together, we can then start to see this in terms of an assemblage, a coming together of language (including translingual practice), people and religion (and/or minzu), place (Muslim Street), and objects to provide a particular set of semiotic possibilities. Through this semiotic assemblage belonging is formed on Muslim Street, where the passing on of heritage through food is made possible. In this respect, Yating who had just set up her food delivery business in the area, told me that

> The food in Huifang [the Hui community] should not be lost, nor failed to be passed on to the next generation. In Huifang people are gregarious, and their gregariousness should make our food heritage easy to pass on. But some

traditional dishes, such as the porcelain cake candy (瓷糕糖巴; cígāo tángbā) and lumpy oil tea (疙瘩油茶; gēda yóuchá) are lost and failed to pass on. Some craftsmanship is not inherited.... As for why I started this part of the online business, one reason is because of the epidemic, and the other is because we also want to keep practising our traditional food from the area, to keep these things in Huifang. As far as we can, we hope to preserve it.

As with the Quranic verses of the calligraphers, Arabic letters that have been removed but retain a ghostly visibility are common by-products from heritage literacy in the area. As texts become written over, scraped off, erased, and in some cases forgotten, heritage literacies operate through urban palimpsests which become further layered as time goes on and thus subtly inscribed with plurality. To see them this way requires an acknowledgement of their ideological nature. In some cases, that which is erased is renegotiated, such as when the term 'halal' becomes 'qingzhen', 'Muslim Food' 'Northwest', etc., and heritage practice is renewed and cultural memory revitalised. In other cases, such as in Xing's case, qingzhen becomes forgotten or disregarded. Forms of heritage practice beyond that of food seem to be less amenable to adaptation for many Sino-Muslims (see Bhatt and Wang 2023).

Just like the palimpsests created from layers of the simple strokes of the calligraphers in Section 2, ways of being Sino-Muslim here are through interaction with physical objects, bodily acts, and cultural production. These shop signs, and their broader locales, are stages upon which ordinary Muslims (re-) perform their subjectivities. While the performative nature of Sini calligraphy enables practitioners to embrace their hybridity with one identity not relinquishing the other, food vendors working in public spaces must also engage in their own kind of covert semiosis whether it is via the spectral presence of semi-removed and partially visible Arabic text or deploying their scripture name. Some of this, as we shall see in the coming sections, is beyond linguistic and is heavily dependent on the signifying power of objects. Whatever the case, Sino-Muslim heritage literacy is contingent on the repeated rubbing out and doing again, whether it is by compulsion and the need for re-glossing of Sini calligraphic content on social media, or as in the kind of signage discussed.

Visual Muslimness and Food Packaging

Another aspect of semiotic representation which provides an important area for analysis are the visual representations of Muslimness that occur on Sino-Muslim food packaging. In Figure 14 we see the packaging for 'Thirteen Spices', a famous Chinese brand of spices which originated from the recipes of the famous Sino-Muslim chef Wang Shouyi (originally from Kaifeng, Henan). And, in Figure 15, packaging for a soup from another famous brand

Figure 14 Packaging of the 'Thirteen Spices brand with an image of Wang
Shouyi (photo by author).

Figure 15 Gao Qunsheng is another popular qingzhen brand
(image from taobao.com).

'Gao Qunsheng' (高群生) in which we also see an image of a man in a white
hat[45] often worn by Sino-Muslims though these days rarely seen outside of
mosques and community restaurants.

Though all products are qingzhen, nowhere within the image in Figure 14 is
the term 'qingzhen' (or its metonymic equivalent 'halal') visible on the

---

[45] Sometimes referred to as 'worship hat' (礼拜帽; lǐbài mào).

packaging for this famous Chinese Muslim brand, though it does appear in other brands, including the brand 'Gao Qunsheng' shown in Figure 15. Instead, in Figure 14, the picture of a traditional Muslim man with a beard and white hat dominates. Products from the Thirteen Spices brand once featured labels indicating qingzhen and even the word halal (in Arabic), but these labels have since been removed. Consumers are, however, still aware that this is a famous Muslim brand and this is due to the image of the brand's founder, Wang Shouyi, displayed on all the packaging alongside the phrase 'Time-honored brand'. The white hat[46] is of the type that is usually worn by male Islamic scholars (*ulema*) yet there is no mention of the Islamic background of the father and son founders of the brand, nor the qingzhen ethics that drove its conception and maintained its reputation for so long. Wang Shouyi's image alone depicts reliability and 'time-honoured' Chinese culinary quality with very indirect and visual references to Muslimness and the Sino-Muslim association with qingzhen food.

The Gao Qunsheng (高群生) brand in Figure 15 is similar in terms of how it deploys visual Muslimness. A detailed story of the brand's history is outlined on the company's web pages[47] which boasts recipes from a family lineage going back 800 years in the Hui community, and on one webpage even a banner with the Arabic text 'طعام المسلمين' ('the food of Muslims') alongside the qingzhen label. The phrase 'the food of Muslims' on the webpage is a clear and unambiguous expression of the brand's Muslimness yet such labelling would never be seen in public signage and packaging. The website also shows the company headquarters with signs of both qingzhen and halal written in Arabic; though more recently upon searching the location headquarters on the Chinese site Baidu Maps, I saw that their Arabic signage had been removed. It is precisely these forms of indirectness which link this piece of visual data with what we have discussed already regarding the role of covert semiosis in public places.

White Hats

The white hat of Sino-Muslims is an important semiotic marker, particularly during prayer and food-related activities, and it emerges in more than just visual imagery on food packaging. For example, during a storm in Henan Province in 2021, a popularised post on Chinese social media depicted Sino-Muslim businesses serving free breakfast to fellow Chinese with both male and female staff donning their religious white hats. While the two examples of food packaging

---

[46] The hat here resembles a Middle Eastern fez, though Sino-Muslims are more likely to wear a smaller white hat or 'worship hat' (礼拜帽; lǐbài mào).

[47] See: www.gaoqunsheng.net/post/2020gqsanmsl.html.

previously discussed depict images of Sino-Muslim men in white hats, the images below show that even Sino-Muslim women can also do the same in the context of serving food. The hat is therefore somewhat universal among Sino-Muslims with men's hats as sometimes smaller than those worn by women (Xiaoyan 2011).

Historically, during the Yuan (1279–1368) and Ming (1368–1644) dynasties, observant Sino-Muslim men wore a white turban head covering known as a 'daisitar' (戴斯达尔; dàisīdá'ěr). Later, in the Qing dynasty (1644–1911), white hats became more common, and, since it allows the wearer to cover their head for prayer, it also became known as a worship hat, and worn by both men and women in some communities.

The images in Figures 16–18 are taken at a location within the Litong district of Wuzhong city in the Ningxia Hui Autonomous Region. They were taken by one of the focal participants in the study, Fatima who is born and raised in the area and has grown up around family members and vendors wearing white hats for acts of worship, food-related rituals, and sometimes (albeit rarely in modern times) as part of daily attire.

Like Xi'an's Muslim Street, Litong is also known for its qingzhen food and Sino-Muslim businesses, and was even the site of the second Chinese Muslim Food Festival. In Figures 16 and 17 we can see both male and female Sino-Muslim restaurant staff in Wuzhong wearing the hat both while serving and preparing qingzhen food, and in Figure 18 while at home preparing the food for a wedding. According to some of the project's research participants based in Ningxia, white hats are sometimes worn by both men and married women in daily life, as local participant Fatima tells:

> My grandma wore a white hat most of the time before she passed. Some younger women wear them as one would wear a hijab. I usually wear one at home at a nietie.[48]

The white hat is thus in some ways an important object of material culture which identifies and represents who Sino-Muslims or in modern terms 'the Hui minzu' are in contemporary China. It is recognised by almost all Sino-Muslims, the majority Han, and other ethnic groups as a sign of *who they are*, qingzhen ethics and, more broadly, of Chinese Muslimness. It is a component of religious attire that signifies what Keane (2007, 2018) refers to as semiotic ideologies. These ideologies mediate interconnected practices to prepare the wearer for participative acts of piety, which, as we have already observed, may involve food heritage practices. The concept of semiotic ideologies was discussed in

---

[48] Events of alms giving, as defined at the start of this section.

Figure 16 A male Sino-Muslim restaurant worker in Wuzhong, Ningxia (photo by Fatima and used with permission).

Figure 17 A female Sino-Muslim restaurant worker in Wuzhong, Ningxia (photo by Fatima and used with permission).

Figure 18 A hat is donned by an elderly female as part of a wedding ceremony taking place at home (photo by Fatima and used with permission).

Section 2 and refers to the fundamental beliefs that people hold regarding signs, symbols, and their meanings. This encompasses aspects like the perceived purpose of a sign (such as a white hat), the roles it fulfils, and the potential outcomes that may result from it (in many cases it signals qingzhen ethics). These beliefs are shaped by historical and cultural factors and influence the way people in Sino-Muslim communities use and understand signs and symbols. As such, the white hat holds significance in the study of heritage literacy and must be analysed through its use and interpretation in everyday life. It exists as a node within a complex web of semiotics, encompassing both historical and religious connections. The reason for wearing a white hat, whether for religious worship, to signify qingzhen ethics and authenticity, or ethnic identity, is dependent on its mode of representation and the cultural context in which it is used. For example, Xiaoming from Ningxia uses the white hat as a hypothetical example of what its wearing represents for her and what it suggests about the behaviour of the wearer:

> For me the most important thing about being Hui is not to eat pork, and not to wear a white hat while doing KTV [Karaoke].

When discussing what being Hui means to her, Xiaoming uses the wearing of the white hat as a way to delimit what, in her opinion, a Muslim can and cannot do while wearing it. It thus demonstrates a certain iconicity in the midst of a repertoire of material signifiers of Chinese Muslimness which are socially ascribed and not always about food.

Further to Xiaoming, sensitivity around the white hat was also reported by Min, also from Ningxia, who reports how she does not approve of seeing online posts of Hui women wearing the hat while dancing in public:

> I think there are things, we, as Hui, cannot post online casually. For example, there are posts by some Hui women who wear white hats with skirts and perform dancing. I really dislike those posts. Either you should take off your hats, and if you do wear it, you need to overall dress properly and modestly, and not dance in public. I'm really against that.

While not usually wearing a hat herself, Min expresses its religious importance for her, and dislike of how elements of minzu 'intangible cultural heritage' have, through political policy, been transformed from complex religio-cultural traditions into staged, exoticised, and patriotic 'song and dance' performances for entertaining displays of 'diversity' (see Anonymous 2021). As with the qingzhen signage, the white hat also becomes an object through which multiple, and perhaps at times competing and conflicting, ideologies may come together.

How Sino-Muslim calligraphers, 'qingzhen' food vendors and manufacturers, and others, cultivate an ethical and heritage-rich landscape while tiptoeing shifting red-lines around religious expression is an issue for which the participants in this study continue to search for answers. Added to this is the prospect that their heritage practices can, and do, become stripped of all essence and rendered into meaningless forms of entertainment and tokens of diversity. State-censorship and the related self-censorship of Sino-Muslims is closely intertwined with their own interpretations of shifting state discourses and commitment to religious heritage in everyday life, particularly in maintaining sacred-profane distinctions. This commitment creates a co-evolving ecology of a semiotics of Muslimness that straddles online and offline practices, and thus about far more than marking out halal food as a distinct commodity.

While some of the examples discussed may be fairly localised and idiosyncratic, and others standardised (such as food packing and white hats), the analysis shows that as materialisations they have immense semiotic complexity in their ties to sacredness. Examining how, as semiotic assemblages, words, languages, objects and locales together shape meaning also tells us about how people identify activities and signs as religious, ethnic, or geographical (or a combination thereof). Moreover, this understanding extends to how objects can mark, inscribe, and interpret the past as heritage and the power of signs to construct social realities.

4 Heritage Literacy in Liminal Spaces
Liminality

When we see heritage literacy in broad terms, as any form of meaningful semiotic activity that relates to heritage, then we are faced with the possibility of analysing more kinds of data and in more complex ways. Previous sections of this Element have examined Sino-Muslim heritage literacy in categories that might be deemed as clearly defined or occurring in contexts that are quite readily noticeable in Chinese society. In this section, however, I explore heritage literacy which occupies and appropriates *liminal spaces*. This means that each situation discussed herein evokes some form of *liminality* (from the Latin 'limen'; threshold), a conceptual term that was developed by the cultural anthropologist Victor Turner (1974) in the context of his work on ritual to characterise situations that are neither within one recognised context nor the other (and as such occupying an 'in-between' space). Turner himself had arrived at his view by expanding upon van Gennep's (1909/1960) idea that liminality represents a transitional, temporal experience. Therefore, the examples that I have drawn from in this section could be interpreted as liminal in several ways, including in terms of their occurrence within in-between spaces, states of being and, in the final subsection, even beyond Chinese contexts and the Hui community.

In this respect, in terms of identity, Madison (2005) develops Turner's concept of liminality and uses it to describe 'a state of being neither here nor there – neither completely inside nor outside a given situation, structure or mindset' (Madison 2005, p. 158). Sino-Muslims can live and move through Chinese society with a particular kind of 'double-consciousness' (see Du Bois 1994) that in varying ways allows acknowledgement of their religious heritage while carrying the weight of being under the watchful and censorious gaze of outsiders. Du Bois' (1994) theory of double-consciousness connotes how subordinate or colonised communities navigate social terrains with an awareness of 'always looking at one's self through the eyes of others, of measuring one's soul by the tape of a world that looks on' (p. 45). Liminal spaces are where such internal conflict and simultaneity are most pronounced.

It could be argued that liminality is the sine qua non of Sino-Muslim heritage literacy, and something which undergirds much of what has been discussed already. While liminality is a space for ambiguity and insecurity, it is also a site for the invention, discovery, and creativity of heritage. In this section I employ the concept of liminality to highlight specific characteristics of material conditions and heritage literacy practices which are considered both beyond conventional understandings of heritage and even Sino-Muslim communities themselves. The latter therefore denotes practices which are *conceptually liminal*.

The source material for this section comes from images that the participants shared as part of the research. In preliminary interviews they were asked about the importance and locations of artefacts of heritage literacy in their lives. A significant portion of the following discussion is a result of their responses and subsequent follow-up research encounters that ensued.

Religious Hangings

In Section 2, I discussed how almost any object that is inscribed with Quranic Arabic is considered sacred and imbued with religious significance. In this section, I turn to how respondents often spoke, sometimes at length, about how they engage with different types of religious artwork and hangings in their lives. These decorative works were most often forms of scriptural writing, such as the kind of Quranic calligraphy discussed in Section 2, and in the form of scrolls, 'middle hall' hangings, paper-cuttings, tapestries, or traditional Chinese ceramics. In all cases they were given as gifts or bought to adorn homes and businesses for blessings, spiritual protection, and ways to remind. They thus form an important perspective within the analysis and extend some of the points already raised in previous sections. In this subsection I focus more on the nature as well as the location of these decorative writings and what that tells us about the values and practices associated with these heritage literacy artefacts.

One of the most common places where such hangings and decorative items were located was in family homes. The image in Figure 19 is from Zhiyuan who is from Henan but recently moved to Malaysia for work. In his spare time, he writes on sociology and religion. The image is taken from his home and it shows several pieces of art beside the television, including a ceramic plate and incense burner both with Sini calligraphic motifs, a typical Chinese 'ink wash' painting above, and ceramic vases in the cabinet to the side. About this image he says:

> We have a Chinese painting on the wall alongside an incense burner just below the television, so everyone who comes here can see it. It is advertised proof (标榜证明) that I am from a Chinese Muslim family.

These artefacts have importance for Zhiyuan as imagistic carriers of Islamic script, as we have discussed already. The incense burner, which contains the Islamic declaration of faith in Arabic, is of a design that is widely used across various Chinese rituals and would thus be recognisable to a member of any religious group. The Chinese blue-and-white (青花; qinghua) porcelain decorated with Arabic and Persian writing is a distinctive representation of the Sino-Muslim culture that has developed since Islam was introduced to China during

Figure 19 Zhiyuan's ceramic Sini calligraphy piece beside an incense burner with Chinese ink wash artwork (photo by Zhiyuan and used with permission).

the Tang dynasty. In bygone times these objects were created for the consumption of Muslim elites and illustrate the centuries-long trade between, and combined artistic heritage of, the Chinese and Islamic worlds (Frankel 2018). Being a Chinese expat now living in Malaysia (and therefore in a state of in-betweenness), Zhiyuan positions this front-and-centre in the main room of his home as 'advertised proof' of being both Chinese and Muslim. Mike, from Gansu Province, relates a similar account when asked about the hangings in his home during his childhood:

> Growing up, these hangings served as reminder that I belonged to a different group from the majority Han population, that I have a tradition to inherit and pass on ... We would want our visitors to see we are religious so they were put up in main rooms, so they could see Islamic writings in the house.

When it came to talking about such artefacts, participants such as Zhiyuan and Mike frequently blurred the boundaries between Hui ethnicity and Islamic faith by describing religious art in the home as 'proof' of being Muslim. In Mike's case the hangings served as a reminder to the family primarily that they 'belonged to a different group from the Han majority'. This was also the case with participants within China who used to display Arabic inscriptions upon their front doors also as 'proof of a Hui family'. It was one of the very few instances when the two constructs came together harmoniously in discourse. Furthermore, the practice of wishing to show proof of identity to either fellow Chinese (in most cases Han), or non-Chinese (in Zhiyuan's case, Malaysians) is something that itself bespeaks a way to maintain a sense of liminality – or hybridity – through the hangings.

With time, Mike's family changed the way they viewed the hangings after a period of difficulty:

> Later, we felt that they could protect us from evil. So we started putting them up in the bedrooms. Particularly after my grandpa, in a period of distress, felt that he saw 'devilish beings' in the bedroom.

Here we see that the semiotic ideologies associated with sacred art shifted from one of serving to *remind* the family (as a symbol of ethnic and religious difference from the Han), towards an ever-present emblem of safety and *protection* particularly during times of distress. Semiotic ideologies may not remain constant, therefore. For Zhiyuan, the artefacts are also ways to remind and protect:

> Some people believe that a hanging will ward off evil, but many don't know what is written. To me it is motivating. For example, there is one hanging in my house now which says 'He who glorifies Allāh, Allāh will open up a way out for him'. Such a thing for me is a decoration on the one hand, a little Islamic atmosphere on the other. In my study I have a small room dedicated to worship, and there is a calligraphy hanging of the three Quranic surahs for protection[49] to remind me to focus.

Zhiyuan caveats his belief that a hanging can serve to protect with an ability to read what is written in the art itself; for him it is less *emblematic* and more *hermeneutic*. In light of his point about artefacts embodying 'a little Islamic atmosphere', further exploration of where such artefacts tend to be located is necessary. In better understanding this, we may need to look beyond the home and into spaces that are better considered as 'semi-public'. For example, cars and everyday personal objects.

Out of Sight but Not Mind

The government's increased control over religious expression in public spaces has caused individuals to make strategic decisions regarding their daily religious practices. As a result, personal choices and community activities are constantly shaped through negotiation and adaptation. Based on what has

---

[49] This relates to the last three suras in the Quran (chapters 112, 113 and 114).

Figure 20 Fatima's Quranic hanging in the car (photo by Fatima and used with permission).

been discussed already, Sino-Muslims, by and large, do not view Arabisation or sinicisation as conflicting paths for maintaining their faith. Instead, they have demonstrated their versatility by creatively combining aspects of their identities through the performance of such things as Sini calligraphy and food heritage practices. However, curbs on religious expression in public spaces have also impacted some private spaces. For example, in Figure 20 we can see a Quranic hanging which belongs to Fatima who is based in Wuzhong (Ningxia Hui Autonomous Region). About this she told us that

> The car is the only place where the family can have a religious symbol. Since some of my family members are political officials, we are not allowed any religious books or symbols in our possession within the home. This is checked often. So I have to keep this is my car.

Fatima's placing of the Quranic hanging in the car suggests one of many 'performative tactics' (Wang 2019a, p. 86) of China's Sino-Muslims. It shows an attempt to evade rules that infringe upon personal space (inside her home, since her family are political officials), and the manipulation of a liminal space (a car; nether home nor work) in which this practice occurs. In Wang's (2019a) account of the performative tactics of the Sino-Muslims of her study, she draws on Michel de Certeau's (1988) notion of the everyday 'tactics' in which an orthodoxy is subverted and the everyday grounds for an alternative discursive position are laid. de Certeau makes a distinction between *strategies*, understood as the domain of the powerful (where space is officialised and norms imposed) and everyday *tactics* (through which spaces are appropriated and manipulated by individuals; de Certeau 1988, pp. 29–30). Fatima's tactic to make a display of religious expression is not highly calculated and nor does it require much effort. Wang (2019a, pp. 87–88) further suggests about such kinds of performative tactics:

> When an ordinary person of faith carefully selects her forms of displaying piety in public, it is a tactical response to the structural sociopolitical power field in which she lives. But her choice does not necessarily grow out of resistance to the system. She is highly aware of the possible consequences of the choices she makes.

The following examples bespeak everyday performative tactics to make semiosis visible, though not all attempts are successful. Responding to tightening online censorship is one such area, linked closely to the government's growing demand for sinicisation.

Figure 21 shows a post from the Weixin account of Mike, a participant from Gansu Province. The post on his account is about an article from his official account which kept getting removed by censors. In his official account he wrote posts on contemporary Islamic themes, and the article cited in the post was

Figure 21 Mike's Weixin post that kept getting removed (used with permission).

uploaded multiple times in different ways yet kept getting deleted by the Weixin censorship system.

Every post on Weixin, or any article in one of its official accounts, must pass ex ante censorship barriers which are the combined effects of both algorithmic censors (the platform's artificial intelligence) and human censors (human employees). One of the key causes of censorship activation are forms of 'taboo' or 'sensitive' word detection which tends to be focused on words related to politically threatening topics, perceived advocacy for religion (Miller 2018), and events deemed inimical to social harmony. The precise list of which words are sensitive is not clear and considered to constantly evolve, as well as vary among Chinese platforms (Ye and Zhao 2023). Therefore, posting online or even sending a message becomes a process of guesswork, experimentation, and recoding to bypass censorship. Eventual societal normalisation of wide-scale censorship (see Yang 2021) leads to its acceptance and ultimately forms of 'self-censorship', such as what we saw in Section 2 with the calligraphers talking about their work on Weixin. Mike's examples, however, are all forms of *post hoc* censorship as he sought (but ultimately failed) to bypass the detection, leading to his official account eventually becoming blocked shortly after this post.

We can take a closer look at his post to better understand this. It reads (see Figure 16): *I am sorry, it doesn't allow me to post. It doesn't matter if it is video, image or text, or audio, all are disallowed. I wish you peace*, and is followed by a screenshot of the attempts to upload a post named 'How to be an attractive Muslim'. In the first version (timed at 12:15) he writes the post title in full and the accompanying image, text and video, which then becomes blocked moments after he posts it. In the second version (timed at 12:37) he omits the word 'Muslim' (穆斯林; Mùsīlín), as he assumes that this was the sensitive word that triggered the block, and replaces it with 'Mü$lim'. He thus uses the textual stand-ins '$' and 'ü' but this does not work either, as the post is again removed. In the third and final post (timed at 12:48), Mike opted for an audio-only format for his post, and assumed that his face was detected by facial recognition and also may have caused the post's removal. In this iteration, he assumes that it is both text and his face that have triggered the censor. However, that too became removed, though its deletion is not visible at the time of this post. These stages of the iterations of his post represent discourse tactics to attempt to evade detection by making particular assumptions about what triggers the censorship. In order to tip-toe the red line, he needs to know where it is. He further assumes that the censor will not pick up an audio-only post, thinking this would work, but it does not.

Ye and Zhao (2023) describe such strategies as part of Chinese 'sensitive word culture' in which netizens (online users) attempt to voice their opinions through creative discourse strategies to transcend the censorship system. Eventually, some people succeed at it. But Mike did not, and very shortly after this post his account was cancelled. There are many examples of participants' semiotic practices with respect to working within the red lines of online censorship in China. Another example is from Zhiyuan from Henan who, like Mike, occasionally writes articles for his official account, some of which are removed by censors. Echoing Mike's evasion tactics, he tells:

> If my post is removed, I look back and try to think which word was it that triggered the censoring. I then do not use that word again in the next version.

When I asked Mike about adopting a less direct approach in his religious discussions online, he replied:

> In China there are Muslims who adopt a less direct approach. There is an Ahong I know who discusses the Prophet, cites hadiths and the Quran, but he never says 'the Prophet said . . . '[50] he says 'my teacher said . . . ', to avoid censorship. His articles do not get blocked. Personally, I do not agree with this approach.

For both Mike and Zhiyuan, evading censorship is about developing an encrypted language that is neither Chinese nor non-Chinese, and thereby an attempt at creating a liminal space online.

A slightly more creative tactic was talked about by Lei from Xi'an. Lei undertook a traditional scripture hall education and is connected to several Ahongs in the community. He sometimes uses Weixin to ask them religious questions and is also mindful of the platform's policy on religious discourse. When texting one of his Ahong friends with an Islamic question, he says he does the following:

> I type my question, or audio message. Ahong then by hand writes his response on paper, takes a photo of the paper, and sends it to me. I save the image immediately, as he has two minutes in which he can 'recall' his message. If he keeps it over two minutes it stays.

Lei's approach is not to recode what he wants to say with encrypted forms of language but to use a combination of different modes, hand-writing and image,

---

[50] Here Mike recalls the Ahong's use of the term 'shèngrén' (圣人) to denote 'prophet'. This is the term that many Sino-Muslim literati have historically used to describe the Prophet Muhammad. Sino-Muslim portrayal of the Prophet Muhammad as 'the sage from the West' alongside Confucius as 'the sage from the East' (see Ben-Dor Benite 2005, pp. 171–5) allowed them to refer to Muhammad as a part of Chinese tradition and render him a culturally intelligible figure in Han society. However, in this extract, even the historically accepted use of 'sage' must be substituted for 'teacher' so as not to sound too religious. Other commonly used terms for the Prophet of Islam are 先知 (xiānzhī) and 钦圣 (qīn shèng).

to bypass sensitive word detection. Lei was under the perception that if his friend uses the 'recall' function to withdraw the message, a feature released by the Weixin platform in 2014, then the image is not stored in Weixin's data files. It is unclear – and unlikely – that the image as a datum is not stored somewhere, either in Weixin servers or the device's backend, but this is not important to the two of them. What matters is to remove its *prima facie* presence on the device (in case it is checked by someone) and also to avoid their Weixin accounts getting flagged by censorship and banned altogether.

Though Lei, Mike and Zhiyuan all still attempted to *disrupt* the original text while still maintaining comprehensibility, their methods are different. For Lei, an image of a rather roughly hand-written text can be saved in time before his friend recalls the message. It might also seem somewhat ironic that a more old-fashioned hand-written note is a preferred mode of response for his digital query. Lei's example speaks to the 'postdigital' (see Bhatt 2023a, 2023b) nature of online heritage literacy practices, and the development of a semiotic assemblage which is configured through a range of material interests. It is illustrative of how literacy practices are not determined solely by connectivity to the Internet or analogue tools of writing, but through people's situated and contingent practices for getting things done in life, in this case asking his Ahong a religious query. Heritage literacy practices here are individuated, particular and dynamic rather than in line with a mould of cultural practice, and only really graspable in the emergent semiotic assemblage.

These examples of attempts at evasion and recoding are the ordinary 'tactics' (de Certeau 1988) in the everyday life of many Internet users in China. Such practices have been particularly salient for ordinary Muslims in China today owing to intensified practices of digital surveillance dovetailed with various forms of anti-Muslim sentiments (Wang 2019a). Echoing Ye and Zhao (2023), the practices outlined are much more than simply 'repression versus resistance'. Rather, Sino-Muslim use of the Chinese social media platforms becomes a site of subtly negotiated boundaries between the sacred and the profane in everyday life, though sometimes this boundary occurs within words and semiotic artefacts themselves. How this negotiation occurs informs our understanding of how a semiotics of Muslimness connects closely to navigating sensitive word detection as an evolving cultural practice amongst Chinese netizens.

A Qingzhen Tea Ceremony

Another interesting example of a semiotics of Muslimness which has occurred through the course of this research is one that I encountered both outside of China and of Sino-Muslim communities themselves. During a research visit to

Türkiye, I came across a diverse group of Muslims (mostly Chinese, Japanese, and Turkish) who undertook a traditional East Asian tea ceremony embellished with artefacts of Islamic religious significance, including Sino-Muslim poetry and calligraphy. I would deem this eclectic practice as 'liminal' in slightly different ways to the examples discussed earlier in this section, and also as potentially significant as a new adaptation of heritage practice that is beyond China and the Hui community.

The traditional East Asian tea ceremony, also known as the Way of Tea (茶道; chádào), is a ritual that originated in China and was later adopted by Japan and Korea (Okakura 2010). The ceremony is rooted in ancient East Asian mythology, and steeped in a metaphysics that emphasises the balance and harmony of the universe. At its core, the tea ceremony is not just a simple act of making and serving tea but a way to cultivate mindfulness and harmony through meditating on the transient nature of existence.

In the early periods of the practice in Japan (and before that in Tang era China), there were Zen Buddhist and Taoist tea ceremonies, a Samurai tea ceremony and later a Catholic tea ceremony, as the practice became appropriated by those who wished to use its metaphysics as a means to express their religion or other type of belief. Various appropriations over the centuries have been fairly easy to achieve as the tea ceremony involves flower arrangement, calligraphy, poetry, a tearoom, and of course tea itself.

In the study, I engaged with the group and interviewed its founder Naoki Yamamoto[51] (see Yamamoto 2022) who outlined his motivations for founding the practice in Turkey as follows:

> Some students in Turkey asked me to introduce them to authentic East Asian cultural practices. At the time I was undertaking a course in the Urasenke School of Tea, so I brought the Japanese tea ceremony utensils and explained the process to the students. I undertook a kind of Islamic 'semantic reconstruction' of the ceremony, by using Islamic terms alongside the Japanese terms such as *murshid* for sensei (guide), *silsila* for keihu (chain of masters), *ijaza* for kyojou (formal authorisation), *alam al kabir* for dai uchuu (macrocosmos), and *alam al saghir* for sho uchuu (micro-cosmos).

Naoki tells how he undertook a 'semantic reconstruction' of the tea ceremony by using Islamic and Japanese terminology alongside each other in the tea ceremony. For Naoki this is to demonstrate commonalities in the cosmology, metaphysics, theology and spiritual psychology of both Teaism and Islam. He takes the semantic reconstruction further:

---

[51] Though anonymity is an important tenet of the ethical procedures for the study, in this instance Naoki preferred to keep his identity known. I thereby created an exception in this case and modified the study protocols accordingly.

> To me, the blackness of the tea represents the purified state of the soul or '*nafs al mutma'inna*' [the soul at rest[52]] and the removal of worldly distractions, '*al khawatir*'. I also began to call it a 'qingzhen' tea ceremony to reflect the Chinese Muslim essence, and I use the Japanese pronunciation of the same Chinese characters 'seishin' (清真).

In the previous extract Naoki mentions how he has used the Chinese term 'qingzhen' to describe the tea ceremony, to reflect both its Chinese links and Islamic inflection. Referring to it as the 'qingzhen tea ceremony' is further substantiated by the incorporation of Sino-Muslim texts as per his account:

> In the tea ceremony, first the students bow to the hanging scroll, which usually contains a philosophical message. I use various poems from Chinese Islamic heritage including Liu Zhi's poem about the microcosm and macrocosm. I think it reflects the ceremony's philosophy very well. I also use the traditional Japanese fan, as this is a symbol of the border that demarcates the material and nonmaterial worlds. The fans are also inscribed with Sino-Muslim poetry. The student puts the fan in front of the master and bows. Otherwise, they keep the fan with them to remind them of the tea ceremony's philosophy, and also attempt to learn the poem written on it.

The group encountered in the course of the research conducted the ceremony with the fan depicted in Figure 22, which contains a famous poem on the articles of Islamic belief by the renowned Sino-Muslim theologian Liu Zhi (d. 1724; also discussed in Section 2). The Master (Naoki) in this case issues the fan to his students in order that they hold onto it, memorise the poem inscribed upon it, and learn the points of religious belief via the ceremonial manners of Teaism. Importantly, the poem is in traditional Chinese characters and can therefore be read by both the Japanese and Chinese within the group. Naoki further told me:

> I have designed the fan for myself and my students to feel closer to the East Asian Islamic tradition, and to memorise a classical Islamic Chinese poem to revive the literacy of our tradition. In the past, we [Japanese and Chinese] were both considered part of the same civilisation and sharing the same literacy heritage.

Naoki's small, but growing, troupe of tea ceremony enthusiasts represents an example of a practice which attempts to bring together Chinese Muslim literature, theology, and the ancient practice of serving tea and nurturing etiquette. The group's practice is far removed from China, and the Hui Sino-Muslim community who, as far as I have found, have not incorporated the tea ceremony as a delineated

---

[52] This refers to the state of person who has overcome their fleshly appetites, according to Al-Ghazali's (d. 1111) philosophy of mind in which he outlines four dimensions of 'the self' in his 'The Marvels of the Heart' (see Skellie 2010).

Figure 22 Tea ceremony fan with Liu Zhi's poem inscribed (photo by author).

heritage practice. Despite inquiries within the research process, I have not encountered any indication of a Sino-Muslim tea ceremony within China, yet the community managed to incorporate aspects of Chinese Kung Fu (Hallenberg 2002), the structural features of Chinese design within mosques (Steinhardt 2018) and Taoist and Confucianist terminology to express Islamic theological concepts (Murata 2000). The spiritual affinity between the East Asian tea ceremony and Islam is made through various Sino-Muslim hanging scrolls and descriptive terms which constitute Naoki's 'semantic reconstruction' of the practice.

The tea ceremony practitioners are important to this analysis because many of the group are not ethnically Hui, and some are even Japanese and Middle Eastern but able – or learning – to read traditional Chinese characters as part of what Naoki describes as 'the same literacy heritage'. The group's use of Liu Zhi's poem and other calligraphic artefacts form part of what could be seen as an adapted form of Sino-Muslim heritage practice. The group members are thus contemporary purveyors of Sino-Muslim heritage who are not following an existing mould of cultural practice that is considered to be a part of 'the way things have been done', as with the other participants of this study. Rather, they are undertaking new forms of cultural production as a community that is neither traditionally Sino-Muslim (i.e. Hui) or within China.

The tea ceremony's heritage value emerges through a mixture of the aesthetic, sensory, metaphysical, and textual. It thus fits with Harrison's (2015) conception of heritage as less about preserving that which might be lost without efforts of conservation, and more about a process of 'material-discourse' which is 'collaborative, dialogical and interactive' and through which 'past and future arise out of dialogue and encounter between multiple embodied subjects in (and with) the present' (Harrison 2015, p. 27).

When these mostly new Muslims were asked about the way they conduct the tea ceremony, they replied in ways that express their collective Taoist and Confucianist origins as emphatically East Asian Muslims and not part of the Middle Eastern, South Asian, or South-East Asian communities, who are also known for their love of tea. The Islamic Tea Ceremony is, for them, a form of ontological contemplation as East Asian Muslims residing far from their countries of origin and who are brought together by a common Taoist and Confucianist civilisational root.

In recent times, there has been a surge of Han nationalist sentiment in China. This trend has also given rise to a growing desire among non-Han Chinese to assert their unique cultural identities, and in some cases, even express political differences with Han-centric narratives of Chineseness. This phenomenon shares similarities with Baojie's experience (a Han Muslim convert discussed in Section 2) of embracing Sini calligraphy as a means of identifying with Muslim culture, beyond the confines of official ethnic, or minzu, categories. The underlying theme here is a yearning to associate with a Muslimness that is rooted in Chinese traditions, but not exclusively focused on Han culture. This is accomplished under the banner of 'civilisation', a term discursively invoked by many participants when discussing signs and their significance.

For groups like this, assembling a semiotics of Muslimness in ways that suggest new pathways of heritage literacy is an important form of cultural production. It harks back to an established past through Sini calligraphy and Sino-Muslim theological poetry (among other things), but brings a semiotics of Muslimness to bear outwith China and in ways that might seem alien to Sino-Muslims proper. While the example of the qingzhen tea ceremony in this section may appear somewhat speculative and even outside the scope of this research, I would argue that it sets the ground for further work that could look at *creative adaptations* of heritage literacy practices among the diasporic Chinese Muslim communities, particularly within the Middle East and the Indonesian Archipelago.

5 Conclusions: A Semiotics of Muslimness

Through examining the semiotics of Muslimness across key elements of a broader study into Sino-Muslim heritage literacy, I have attempted to address bigger issues of the ways in which language, digital media, and material culture are used to construct Muslimness as a unique sphere of semiotic practice in China. This Element has attempted to feature different yet synchronically existing semiotic markers highlighted to identify Muslimness in China, and how they are deployed by people in the service of different purposes, be it in expressing religious sentiments in strictly secular domains, demarcating Muslim spaces, verification of halal food and qingzhen ethics, and recent adaptations of heritage literacy beyond China's shores. In all cases, a semiotics of Muslimness exists to serve not just identification strategies, but to also *perform* Muslim or Hui identities in secular China, to differentiate from Han Chineseness, and thereby (re)define the boundaries of ethnic and religious spaces. Ultimately, therefore, heritage practices of various types are confirmed and constituted by the coherence of an assemblage – the intersection of different modes and practices including material artefacts, food, script, alongside other vibrant materials, embodied actions and spatialisations. In turn, together with texts, the interplay of these different semiotic resources produces the construct of heritage as a coherent (aka meaningful; recognisable) *performance* (Goffman 1959).

Goffman's (1959) conception of performance can help elucidate the connection between signs and performativity. Goffman defines performance as 'all the activity of a given participant on a given occasion which serves to influence in any way any of the other participants' (p. 15). The examples discussed in this Element all have the potential for performativity in different ways through various signs which communicate actively to the world: the calligraphic pieces of art and their exegeses; various iterations of qingzhen food signage; depictions of Sino-Muslim men and women in white hats, and much more. All these point to categories of 'performance'.

Also, without the semiotic meanings conveyed by the signs, each performance becomes a very different event that may have little or nothing to do with Sino-Muslim heritage. This is because each sign offers two possible kinds of meaning: One is denotational and is via the apparent and conventional linguistic and semiotic system adopted; the second is connotational and indexical, and rooted in 'sociocultural, political, historical and economic bodies of knowledge and experience' (Blommaert 2015, p. 15). In more practical terms, one meaning effect may denote Hui ethnic heritage and culture, particularly confined within the minzu paradigm. Meanwhile, another may connote a representative symbol for Muslimness that implies that certain practices extend beyond just calligraphy, food, or tea, and resonate deeply within the framework of religious conviction. Rather, they are about forms of Islamic heritage practice which undergird the Hui construction of identity within an ultra-secular Han-dominated society. These practices are characterised by their *simultaneity*, and are also used to contour spaces where certain relations become embedded. They thus become hard to ignore.

The construct of semiotic assemblage has enabled me to acknowledge the translingual, multimodal, and multisensory resources that intersect in particular practices of heritage literacy, giving them their distinct qualities. Through this study, I have come to appreciate how heritage literacy represents a site in which social, linguistic, and political factors converge, shaping the interaction of various elements such as people, their attire, signage, and scriptural art. These elements are crucial resources that contribute to the complex work of a semiotic assemblage in practices of heritage literacy.

Furthermore, attention to semiotic ideologies connects signs with the particular social, cultural, political, and historical circumstances of Sino-Muslims. Semiotic ideology therefore links the ways Sino-Muslims make sense of heritage literacy to their fundamental presuppositions about Muslimness in their own existence, past, present, and prospective future. Values attached to Muslimness, and their cultural and political consequences, are all guided by their respective semiotic ideologies which underlie the study participants' narratives. Variations in ideologies at the level of everyday heritage literacy are what make simultaneity possible, through a continual set of exchanges, conversations, negotiations, and translations.

Heritage literacy thus takes its sociosemiotic power and significance from such constantly evolving circumstances, making it difficult for an outside observer to establish without a commitment to (auto-)ethnographic inquiry. For these reasons, literacy studies, linguistic anthropology, and linguistic ethnography are well placed to engage with the complex semiotic landscape of Sino-Muslim heritage, in ways that extend beyond an exclusively linguistic imaginary and that integrates with its necessary aesthetic, tactile, and spatial modalities.

I also suggest in this Element that Sino-Muslims sometimes used *covert semiosis* to signal identity and Muslimness in ways that were not immediately obvious to all; some practices were only accessible to members of the community and served to reinforce a sense of identity and belonging, as well as delineate difference. By recognising the role of covert semiosis in practices of communication and heritage literacy, researchers can gain a deeper understanding of the complex ways in which meaning is created and negotiated in the social and cultural contexts of minorities.

This research has shown that a semiotics of Muslimness in China is important for two key reasons: First, Sino-Muslims do not live in exclusive regions within China but rather are scattered across the country. They are also often indistinguishable from the majority Han population. Signs and their denotations thus serve as important 'symbolic anchors' to arouse belonging and indicate demarcation in spaces where religious heritage emerges in strictly policed conditions. Second, Sino-Muslims do not have a separate minority language (as do the Mongol and Uighur minorities, for example) through which their religious heritage might be ring-fenced and protected (see Bhatt and Wang 2023). In such conditions the spatial, the religious, and the ethnic are always negotiable and in flux, with new adaptations of heritage literacy and everyday Muslimness in practice as essential points of inquiry. Overall, this study has contributed to theoretical and methodological understandings of how semiotics and heritage literacy operate in complex and diverse cultural contexts, and provides a foundation for future research on the role of signs and their denotations in shaping identity, belonging, and cultural production.

References

Abd-Allah, U. F. (2006). Islam and the Cultural Imperative. *CrossCurrents*, **56** (3), 357–75.

Ahmad, R. (2011). Urdu in Devanagari: Shifting Orthographic Practices and Muslim Identity in Delhi. *Language in Society*, **40** (3), 259–84.

Anonymous (2021). You shall Sing and Dance: Contested 'Safeguarding' of Uyghur Intangible Cultural Heritage. *Asian Ethnicity*, **22** (1), 121–39.

Avni, S. (2014). Hebrew in the North American Linguistic Landscape: Materializing the Sacred. In Spolsky, B., Inbar-Lourie, O. & Tannenbaum, M. (Eds.) *Challenges for Language Education and Policy: Making Space for People* (pp. 196–213). New York: Routledge.

Bai, S. & Yang, Z. (2002). *An Outline History of China*. Beijing: Foreign Languages Press.

Bakhtin, M. M. (1984). *Problems of Dostoevsky's Poetics (trans. Emerson, Caryl)*. Minneapolis: University of Minnesota Press.

Baquedano-López, P. (2016). Socialization into Religious Sensation in Children's Catholic Religious Instruction. In Lytra, V., Volk, D. & Gregory, E. (Eds.) *Navigating Languages, Literacies and Identities* (pp. 81–94). New York: Routledge.

Barad, K. (2007). *Meeting the Universe Halfway: Quantum Physics and the Entanglement of Matter and Meaning*. Durham, NC: Duke University Press.

Barthes, R. (1977). *Image, Music, Text*. London: Flamingo.

Barton, D. (2007). *Literacy: An Introduction to the Ecology of Written Language*. Oxford: Blackwell.

Bauman, R. & Briggs, C. L. (1990). Poetics and Performances as Critical Perspectives on Language and Social Life. *Annual Review of Anthropology*, **19** (1), 59–88.

Ben-Dor Benite, Z. (2005). *The Dao of Muhammad: A Cultural History of Muslims in Late Imperial China*. Cambridge: Harvard University Press.

Bennett, J. (2010). *Vibrant Matter : A Political Ecology of Things*. Durham, NC: Duke University Press.

Benor, S. B. (2020). Bivalent Writing: Hebrew and English Alphabets in Jewish English. *Journal of Jewish Languages*, **8**(1–2), 108–57.

Bhatt, I. (2023a). Postdigital Literacies. In Jandrić, P. (Ed.) *Encyclopedia of Postdigital Science and Education* (pp. 1–5). Cham: Springer Nature Switzerland.

Bhatt, I. (2023b). Postdigital Possibilities in Applied Linguistics. *Postdigital Science and Education*. https://doi.org/10.1007/s42438-023-00427-3.

Bhatt, I. & Wang, H. (2023). Everyday Heritaging: Sino-Muslim Literacy Adaptation and Alienation. *International Journal of the Sociology of Language*, **2023**(281), 77–101.

Blommaert, J. (2005). *Discourse: A Critical Introduction*. Cambridge: Cambridge University Press.

Blommaert, J. (2015). Meaning as a Nonlinear Effect: The Birth of Cool. *AILA Review*, **28** (1), 7–27.

Bourdieu, P. (1986). The Forms of Capital. In Richardson, J. (Ed.) *Handbook of Theory and Research for the Sociology of Education* (pp. 241–58). Westport: Greenwood.

Bucholtz, M. & Hall, K. (2005). Language and Identity. In Duranti, A. (Ed.) *A Companion to Linguistic Anthropology* (pp. 369–94). Oxford: Blackwell.

Canagarajah, A. S. (2013). *Literacy as Translingual Practice: Between Communities and Classrooms*. New York: Routledge.

Certeau, M. de. (1988). *The Practice of Everyday Life: Volume 1*. Berkeley: University of California Press.

Dong, H. (2020). Language Behavior and Identity Change in the Fangshang Hui Community of Xi'an. *Journal of Asian Pacific Communication*, **30** (1–2), 255–72.

Du Bois, W. E. B. (1994). *The Souls of Black Folk*. Avenel: Gramercy Books.

Erie, M. S. (2016). *China and Islam: The Prophet, the Party, and Law*. New York: Cambridge University Press.

Feng, Y. & Bodde, D. (1976). *A Short History of Chinese Philosophy*. New York: Free Press.

Ferber, M. P. (2006). Critical Realism and Religion: Objectivity and the Insider/ Outsider Problem. *Annals of the Association of American Geographers*, **96** (1), 176–81.

Frankel, J. D. (2011). *Rectifying God's Name : Liu Zhi's Confucian Translation of Monotheism and Islamic Law*. Honolulu: University of Hawai\02BFi Press.

Frankel, J. D. (2018). Muslim Blue, Chinese White: Islamic Calligraphy on Ming Blue-and-white Porcelain. *Orientations*, **49** (2), 2–7.

Frankel, J. D. (2021). *Islam in China*. New York: I.B. Tairus-Bloomsbury.

Gan, N. (2018). *How China is Trying to Impose Islam with Chinese Characteristics in the Hui Muslim Heartland, 14 May 2018*. www.scmp.com/news/china/pol icies-politics/article/2145939/how-china-trying-impose-islam-chinese-character istics (cited 23 November 2022).

Gee, J. P. (2008). *Social Linguistics and Literacies: Ideology in Discourses*. London: Routledge.

Gillette, M. B. (2000). *Between Mecca and Beijing: Modernization and Consumption Among Urban Chinese Muslims.* Stanford: Stanford University Press.

Gladney, D. C. (1998). *Ethnic Identity in China: The Making of a Muslim Minority Nationality.* London: Harcourt Brace College Publishers.

Gladney, D. C. (2004). *Dislocating China: Reflections on Muslims, Minorities and Other Subaltern Subjects.* London: Hurst.

Goffman, E. (1959). *The Presentation of Self in Everyday Life.* New York: Anchor Books.

Gourlay, L., Littlejohn, A., Oliver, M. & Potter, J. (2021). Lockdown Literacies and Semiotic Assemblages: Academic Boundary Work in the Covid-19 Crisis. *Learning, Media and Technology, 46* (4), 377–89.

Greco, C. (2022). Food Heritage, Memory and Cultural Identity in Saudi Arabia: The Case of Jeddah. In Stano, S. & Bentley, A. (Eds.) *Food for Thought: Nourishment, Culture, Meaning* (pp. 55–74). Cham: Springer.

Gumperz, J. H. & Hymes, D. (1972). *Directions in Sociolinguistics the Ethnography of Communication.* New York: Holt, Rinehart and Winston.

Ha, G. (2020). Specters of Qingzhen: Marking Islam in China. *Sociology of Islam, 8* (3–4), 423–47.

Hallenberg, H. (2002). Muslim Martial Arts in China: Tangping (Washing Cans) and Self-defence. *Journal of Muslim Minority Affairs, 22* (1), 149–75.

Harrison, R. (2013). *Heritage: Critical Approaches.* Milton Park, Abingdon: Routledge.

Harrison, R. (2015). Beyond 'Natural' and 'Cultural' Heritage: Toward an Ontological Politics of Heritage in the Age of Anthropocene. *Heritage & Society, 8* (1), 24–42.

Heath, S. B. (1983). *Ways with Words: Language, Life, and Work in Communities and Classrooms.* Cambridge: Cambridge University Press.

Ho, W.-Y. (2018). Digital Islam Across the Greater China: Connecting Virtual Ummah to the Chinese-speaking Muslim Netizens. In Travagnin, S. (Ed.) *Religion and Media in China: Insights and Case Studies from the Mainland, Taiwan and Hong Kong* (pp. 187–202). New York: Routledge.

Irvine, J. T. & Gal, S. (2009). Language Ideology and Linguistic Differentiation. In Duranti, A. (Ed.) *Linguistic Anthropology: A Reader* (pp. 402–34). Malden: Wiley-Blackwell.

Israeli, R. (1997). Translation as Exegesis: The Opening Sūra of the Qur'ān in Chinese. In Riddell, P. G. and Street, T. (Eds.) *Islam: Essays on Scripture, Thought and Society: A Festschrift in Honour of Anthony H. Johns* (pp. 81–103). Leiden: Brill.

Ivanič, S., Laven, M. & Morrall, A. (2019). Introduction. In Morrall, A., Laven, M. & Ivanic, S. (Eds.) *Religious Materiality in the Early Modern World* (pp. 15–32). Amsterdam: Amsterdam University Press.

Keane, W. (2007). *Christian Moderns: Freedom and Fetish in the Mission Encounter*. Berkeley: University of California Press.

Keane, W. (2018). On Semiotic Ideology. *Signs and Society*, **6** (1), 64–87.

Kell, C. (2015). 'Making People Happen': Materiality and Movement in Meaning-Making Trajectories. *Social Semiotics*, **25** (4), 423–45.

Kell, C. (2017). Tracing Trajectories as Units of Analysis for the Study of Social Processes: Addressing Mobility and Complexity in Sociolinguistics. *Text & Talk*, **37** (4), 531–51.

Kong, L. (2001). Mapping 'New'Geographies of Religion: Politics and Poetics in Modernity. *Progress in Human Geography*, **25** (2), 211–33.

Kwo, D.-W. (1990). *Chinese Brushwork in Calligraphy and Painting: Its History, Aesthetics, and Techniques*. London: Constable.

Landry, R. & Bourhis, R. (1997). Linguistic Landscape and Ethnolinguistic Vitality: An Empirical Study. *Journal of Language and Social Psychology*, **16** (1), 23–49.

Leppänen, S., Kytölä, S., Jousmäki, H., Peuronen, S. & Westinen, E. (2014). Entextualization and Resemiotization as Resources for Identification in Social Media. In Seargeant, P. & Tagg, C. (Eds.) *The Language of Social Media: Identity and Community on the Internet* (pp. 112–36). London: Palgrave Macmillan.

Leslie, D., Yang, D. & Youssef, A. (2006). *Islam in Traditional China: A Bibliographical Guide*. Sankt Augustin: Monumenta Serica Institut.

Lipman, J. N. (1997). *Familiar Strangers: A History of Muslims in Northwest China*. Seattle: University of Washington Press.

Ma, H. & Newlon, B. (2022). 10 Praising the Prophet Muḥammad in Chinese: A New Translation and Analysis of Emperor Zhu Yuanzhang's Ode to the Prophet. In Tyeer, S. B. and Gallien, C. (Eds.) *Islam and New Directions in World Literature* (pp. 271–94). Edinburgh: Edinburgh University Press.

Madison, D. S. (2005). *Critical Ethnography: Method, Ethics, and Performance*. London: Sage.

Madsen, R. (2020). Religious Policy in China. In Feuchtwang, S. (Ed.) *Handbook on Religion in China* (pp. 17–33). Cheltenham: Edward Elgar.

Martin-Jones, M. & Jones, K. (2000). *Multilingual Literacies: Reading and Writing Different Worlds*. Amsterdam: J. Benjamins.

Miller, B. (2018). *Delegated Dictatorship: Examining the State and Market Forces Behind Information Control in China [PhD thesis]*. University of Michigan, Ann Arbor.

Mullaney, T. S. (2011). *Coming to Terms with the Nation: Ethnic Classification in Modern China*. Berkeley, Calif.; London: University of California Press.

Murad, A. H. (2020). *Travelling Home: Essays on Islam in Europe*. Cambridge: The Quilliam Press.

Murata, S. (2000). *Chinese Gleams of Sufi Light: Wang Tai-yü's Great Learning of the Pure and Real and Liu Chih's Displaying the Concealment of the Real Realm*. Albany: SUNY Press.

Okakura, K. (2010). *The Book of Tea*. London: Penguin.

Pahl, K. & Rowsell, J. (2011). The Material and the Situated: What Multimodality and New Literacy Studies Do for Literacy Research. In Lapp, D. & Fisher, D. (Eds.) *Handbook of Research on Teaching the English Language Arts* (pp. 175–81). New York: Routledge.

Peirce, C. S. (1934). *Collected Papers of Charles Sanders Peirce: Vol. 5 : Pragmatism and Pragmaticism*. Cambridge: Belknap Press of Harvard University Press.

Pennycook, A. (2017). Translanguaging and Semiotic Assemblages. *International Journal of Multilingualism*, **14** (3), 269–82.

Pennycook, A. (2018). *Posthumanist Applied Linguistics*. London: Routledge.

Petersen, K. (2018). *Interpreting Islam in China: Pilgrimage, Scripture, and Language in the Han Kitab*. New York: Oxford University Press.

Qurratulain, A. & Zunnorain, S. (2015). Acculturation Through Means of Communication: A Study of Linguistic Exchanges Between Chinese and Arabic. *Trames Journal of the Humanities and Social Sciences*, **19** (1), 51–71.

Ridgeon, L. (2020). The Problems of Sinicizing Beijing's Mosques. *Journal of Muslim Minority Affairs*, **40** (4), 576–96.

Rosowsky, A. (2008). *Heavenly Readings: Liturgical Literacy in a Multilingual Context*. Bristol: Multilingual Matters.

Rumsby, S. & Eggert, J. P. (2023). Religious Positionalities and Political Science Research in 'the Field' and Beyond: Insights from Vietnam, Lebanon and the UK. *Qualitative Research*, https://doi.org/10.1177/14687941231165884.

Rumsey, S. K. (2010). Faith in Action: Heritage Literacy as a Synchronisation of Belief, Word and Deed. *Literacy*, **44** (3), 137–43.

Saldaña, J. (2011). *Fundamentals of Qualitative Research*. New York: Oxford University Press.

Sarroub, L. K. (2002). In-betweenness: Religion and Conflicting Visions of Literacy. *Reading Research Quarterly*, **37** (2), 130–48.

Schimmel, A. (1984). *Calligraphy and Islamic Culture*. London: Tauris.

Scollon, R. & Scollon, S. B. K. (2003). *Discourses in Place: Language in the Material World*. London: Routledge.

Scribner, S. & Cole, M. (1981). *The Psychology of Literacy*. Cambridge: Harvard University Press.

Sebeok, T. A. (1976). *Contributions to the Doctrine of Signs*. Bloomington: Indiana University Press.

Shandler, J. (2006). *Adventures in Yiddishland: Postvernacular Language & Culture*. Berkeley: University of California.

Shohamy, E. G., Ben Rafael, E. & Barni, M. (2010). *Linguistic Landscape in the City*. Bristol: Multilingual Matters.

Shohamy, E. G. & Gorter, D. (2009). *Linguistic Landscape: Expanding the Scenery*. New York: Routledge.

Silverstein, M. (2003). Indexical Order and the Dialectics of Sociolinguistic Life. *Language & Communication*, **23** (3), 193–229.

Silverstein, M. & Urban, G. (Eds.). (1996). *Natural Histories of Discourse*. Chicago: The University of Chicago Press.

Skellie, J. W. (2010). *Book of the Explanation of the Marvels of the Heart [Translation of 'Kitab sharh `aja'ib al-qalb']*. Louisville: Fos Vitae.

Steinhardt, N. S. a. (2018). *China's Early Mosques*. Edinburgh: Edinburgh University Press.

Street, B. V. (1984). *Literacy in Theory and Practice*. Cambridge: Cambridge University Press.

Stroup, D. R. (2022). *Pure and True: The Everyday Politics of Ethnicity for China's Hui Muslims*. Seattle: University of Washington Press.

Thum, R. (2018). The Uyghurs in Modern China. In *Oxford Research Encyclopedia of Asian History*. New York: Oxford University Press. https://oxfordre.com/asianhistory/display/10.1093/acrefore/9780190277727.001.0001/acrefore-9780190277727-e-160

Turner, V. W. (1974). *The Ritual Process: Structure and Anti-structure*. Harmondsworth: Penguin.

Tusting, K. (2013). Literacy Studies as Linguistic Ethnography. *Working Papers in Urban Language and Literacies*, **Paper 105**.

van Gennep, A. (1909/1960). *The Rites of Passage*. London: Routledge and Kegan Paul.

Veg, S. A. (2019). *Minjian: The Rise of China's Grassroots Intellectuals*. New York: Columbia University Press.

Wang, J. (2001). *Glossary of Chinese Islamic Terms*. Richmond, Surrey: Curzon [on behalf of the Nordic Institute of Asian Studies].

Wang, J. (2019a). Writing in Palimpsests: Performative Acts and Tactics in Everyday Life of Chinese Muslims. In: Bock, JJ., Fahy, J., Everett, S. (eds)

Emergent Religious Pluralisms. *Palgrave Studies in Lived Religion and Societal Challenges*. Cambridge, UK: Palgrave Macmillan. https://doi.org/10.1007/978-3-030-13811-0_4.

Wang, J. (2019b). Tiptoeing Along the Red Lines. *Terrain [En ligne]*, **72**.

Wang, J. (2022). Networked Islamic Counterpublic in China: Digital Media and Chinese Muslims during Global Pandemic of COVID-19. *New Media & Society*, https://doi.org/10.1177/14614448221095437.

Weixin. (2021). *Administrative Measures for Internet Religious Information Services*. https://mp.weixin.qq.com/s/JB05sFIaikFq-H8v9Dg5RQ (accessed 1 March 2022).

Xiaoyan, W. (2011). The Headscarf and Hui Identity. *Fashion Theory*, **15** (4), 481–501.

Xinhua. (2019). *Mandarin Chinese Promoted to Reduce Poverty*. www.xinhua net.com/english/2019-10/16/c_138476882.htm (accessed 1 February 2023).

Yamamoto, N. (2022). *Is it Possible to Create a Japanese Islamicate Culture?* https://traversingtradition.com/2022/12/12/is-it-possible-to-create-a-japan ese-islamicate-culture/ [Accessed 13 February 2023].

Yang, H. (1981). *Essays on the History of the Hui Nationality [huízú shǐlùn gâo]*. Yinchuan City: Ningxia People's Publisher.

Yang, T. (2021). Normalization of Censorship: Evidence from China [Working paper]. SSRN: https://ssrn.com/abstract=3835217 or http://dx.doi.org/10.2139/ssrn.3835217.

Ye, W. & Zhao, L. (2023). 'I Know it's Sensitive': Internet Censorship, Recoding, and the Sensitive Word Culture in China. *Discourse, Context & Media*, **51**, 100666.

Acknowledgements

I am indebted to the research team who were extremely well placed in doing their part. They are (surname first): Wang Heng (Wahida), Han Xiaofeng (Nuhha), He Jia (Fatima), Tam Yuen Yee (Mariam), Zhang Bowen, and Ni Jianzhou. We all worked very well together and their contribution influenced much of this work. The research would also not be possible without the participants who allowed us into their spaces and generously shared much about their personal lives. I am also grateful to: my funder, the Leverhulme Trust; my institution, Queen's University Belfast; and my Chinese language teacher Chen Jikejia.

I have benefitted greatly from the knowledge, critique, and friendship of Lesley Gourlay, Tarik Elyas and Sadia Khan who read and commented upon drafts. I am also grateful to the following people for their advisory support: Dong Neng, Ma Haiyun, Wang Haichao, Tian Ye, and Naoki Yamamoto.

Cambridge Elements ≡

Applied Linguistics

Li Wei
University College London

Li Wei is Chair of Applied Linguistics at the UCL Institute of Education, University College London (UCL), and Fellow of Academy of Social Sciences, UK. His research covers different aspects of bilingualism and multilingualism. He was the founding editor of the following journals: *International Journal of Bilingualism* (Sage), *Applied Linguistics Review* (De Gruyter), *Language, Culture and Society* (Benjamins), *Chinese Language and Discourse* (Benjamins) and *Global Chinese* (De Gruyter), and is currently Editor of the *International Journal of Bilingual Education and Bilingualism* (Taylor and Francis). His books include the *Blackwell Guide to Research Methods in Bilingualism and Multilingualism* (with Melissa Moyer) and *Translanguaging: Language, Bilingualism and Education* (with Ofelia Garcia) which won the British Association of Applied Linguistics Book Prize.

Zhu Hua
University College London

Zhu Hua is Professor of Language Learning and Intercultural Communication at the UCL Institute of Education, University College London (UCL) and is a Fellow of Academy of Social Sciences, UK. Her research is centred around multilingual and intercultural communication. She has also studied child language development and language learning. She is book series co-editor for *Routledge Studies in Language and Intercultural Communication* and *Cambridge Key Topics in Applied Linguistics*, and Forum and Book Reviews Editor of *Applied Linguistics* (Oxford University Press).

About the Series

Mirroring the *Cambridge Key Topics in Applied Linguistics*, this Elements series focuses on the key topics, concepts and methods in Applied Linguistics today. It revisits core conceptual and methodological issues in different subareas of Applied Linguistics. It also explores new emerging themes and topics. All topics are examined in connection with real-world issues and the broader political, economic and ideological contexts.

Cambridge Elements ☰

Applied Linguistics

Elements in the series

Viral Discourse
Edited by Rodney H. Jones

Second Language Pragmatics
Wei Ren

Kongish: Translanguaging and the Commodification of an Urban Dialect
Tong King Lee

Metalinguistic Awareness in Second Language Reading Development
Sihui Echo Ke, Dongbo Zhang and Keiko Koda

Crisis Leadership: Boris Johnson and Political Persuasion during the Covid Pandemic
Philip Seargeant

Writing Banal Inequalities: How to Fabricate Stories Which Disrupt
Edited by Hannah Cowan and Alfonso Del Percio

New Frontiers in Language and Technology
Christopher Joseph Jenks

Multimodality and Translanguaging in Video Interactions
Maria Grazia Sindoni

A Semiotics of Muslimness in China
Ibrar Bhatt

A full series listing is available at: www.cambridge.org/EIAL.

Printed in the United States
by Baker & Taylor Publisher Services